Eating
&
Cheating

Eating & Cheating

Simple shortcuts,
family meals and fun
recipes for women who
want to live well, cook
more and spend less
time in the kitchen . . . this is
your life on a plate

GILL HOLCOMBE

HODDER &
STOUGHTON

First published in Great Britain in 2010 by Hodder & Stoughton
An Hachette UK company

1

A CIP catalogue record for this title is available from the British
Library

ISBN 978 0 340 99466 5

Illustrations by Hennie Haworth

Design by Annabel Rooker

Typeset in PMN Caecilia and Angelina

Printed and bound by Clays Ltd, St Ives PLC

Hodder & Stoughton policy is to use papers that are natural,
renewable and recyclable products and made from wood grown
in sustainable forests. The logging and manufacturing processes
are expected to conform to the environmental regulations of the
country of origin.

Hodder & Stoughton Ltd
338 Euston Road
London NW1 3BH

www.hodder.co.uk

Eating: 1. the fundamental ingestion of food for survival. 2. Variously living well, dying by chocolate, having your chips, watching your weight, indulging and consoling self, and feeding other people by way of friendship, fondness, or true love. **Cheating**: the best, if not the only way to abide by all of the above.

Contents

Foreword

When you walk into a bookshop and see how many cookery books there are, it's hard to believe anyone will ever write another one, and judging by the number of cookery books most of us own, it's hard to believe anyone will ever **buy** another one.

They used to say everyone has a novel in them. These days it's more likely to be a cookery book. New titles appear every month, hundreds are on sale in stores and supermarkets and hundreds more can be found at car boot sales and in charity shops, many of them now sadly out of print. And that's not counting homemade scrapbooks and ring-bound books put together by groups of people raising money for their communities. Some people love cookery books because they love cooking. Some just like looking at the pictures. But with so many recipes, so many different styles, so many chefs, celebrities, keen amateurs and so much cooking on TV, maybe our insatiable appetite for books about food isn't so surprising.

Someone I know still has around 2,500 cookery books – since she donated her least favourite 500 to the local library – and I recently met a grandmother who told me that when she got engaged, many, many years ago, her father tried to warn her husband-to-be about her shortcomings in the kitchen. 'You do know she can't cook?' said the father. 'But can she read?' said the boy, 'then I'll buy her a book.'

Gill Holcombe

Introduction

When somebody asked me what I usually cook for lunch on Easter Sunday, the question took me by surprise. I can't say for sure what I cooked for lunch on Easter Sunday last year, or any time in the past few years. And I've got no idea what I'll be cooking for lunch next Easter, or the one after that.

When my children were young, what I cooked or didn't cook depended on who was at home and what was happening on the day. One of them could have been staying with cousins (or vice versa), at a friend's house, doing a sports camp or playing in a tournament. Or down with the flu.

Now they're older, they might be out working all day. Or just out all day. A vegetarian may be coming for lunch or the fussy girlfriend who only eats chicken, carrot sticks, skinless cucumber and tomatoes without the pips. And lunch can turn out to be dinner if a big meal in the middle of the day doesn't suit everyone.

If I'm feeling traditional, Easter Sunday lunch could be roast lamb or even turkey with all the trimmings. If I'm halfway through painting the kitchen, it could be takeaway fish and chips (these days, especially in London where I live, anything's possible).

Then there's the timing and the weather to think about. If Easter falls in wet and windy March, we definitely won't be eating outside, but by the latter part of April, it might be warm and sunny. Maybe we'll have a barbecue.

In fact, there's only one day in the year when I can say for certain what I'll be doing for lunch, and even that's pushing it. If we're invited somewhere else for Christmas, I hope I won't be cooking at all.

Recently, somebody else asked me why anyone would make pastry and bread from scratch one day and open a tin of potatoes rather than peel a few fresh ones the next. But why wouldn't they? It seems completely normal to me.

Some women don't cook at all if they can help it. Others turn out better meals than a Michelin-starred chef pretty much all the time. I'm lost in admiration for both extremes, but I suspect that most of us don't conform to either one – or to any other female stereotype. We're a little bit of each, depending on the timing, the children, the weather, the way we feel . . . and everything.

I'm not a fanatical healthy eater or a passionate foodie, but I do love food, and sometimes I love cooking. For me, it's about matching the food to the mood, cooking from scratch when you can, and cheating when you can't. That's what this book is all about.

Cook's Notes

Quantities The quantities of most of the ingredients, especially in the recipes for family meals, can be adjusted to suit you. Specific quantities are only included for one of the following reasons:

- As a starting point for anyone who hasn't cooked the dish before.
- Because it's helpful to know in advance how many portions you can expect to make with a certain volume of food or liquid.
- The amount of any ingredient in the recipe will directly affect the end result.

Servings An indication of how many people each recipe serves is always given for family meals and main dishes. However, in cases where even a rough guide is too general – for desserts, drinks, cake and bread recipes for example – none is included.

Weights and Measures I still think in pounds, ounces and inches rather than metric, especially when I'm cooking, which is why the imperial measurements always come first in the recipes. Pre-packed mince is usually sold in packets of 400g to 500g. It won't matter which size you use unless stated in the recipe.

Mugs Some recipes contain a 'mug' measurement. This is in cases where quantities only need to be approximate and you may not want to bother with scales. As a general guide, in this book one mug = ½ pint (275ml).

Eggs These are medium unless a recipe specifies another size.

Spices Curry and chilli powder are medium unless another degree of heat is specified in the recipe.

Butter and Oil The amount of butter and oil you use for frying etc is up to you. (To me, a generous amount would be about 1oz (25g).) I use one or the other, or a combination of the two, but if you have another preference, that's fine.

Tins Where a 'standard tin' is mentioned, this refers to the average, most common size, although the measurement given on the tin could say 410g, 400ml or 14oz. Where a recipe mentions just 'a tin', this either refers to the standard size or it means the quantity simply doesn't matter, so you can use any size tin you like.

Cake tins To 'long-strip-line' a cake tin, cut one long piece of greaseproof paper or baking parchment to go across the bottom of the tin and up two of the sides, leaving about an inch (2.5cm) of surplus sticking up above the edge. This makes it easy to lift the cake straight out of the tin after cooking.

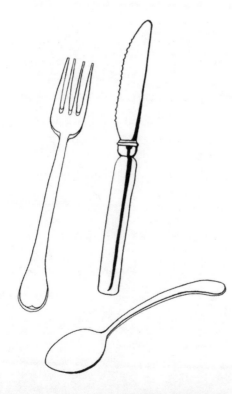

Yummy

'1. Delightful, delicious, very pleasing; especially to taste.
2. Ladies who (cook) lunch, have their cake, and eat it.'

Some women have super-rich husbands, matching children and a servant in every room. But why should they have all the fun?

Yummy isn't a lifestyle in this book, it's a state of mind, whether you want something delicious and nutritious for lunch, healthier biscuits or an absolutely fabulous dessert for no reason at all.

Even if you're more dinner lady than domestic goddess, these recipes are well within your capabilities (and budget) and most of them can be whipped up in less time than it takes to fake an all-over tan and crack open a bottle of special-offer sparkling wine. *Yummy.*

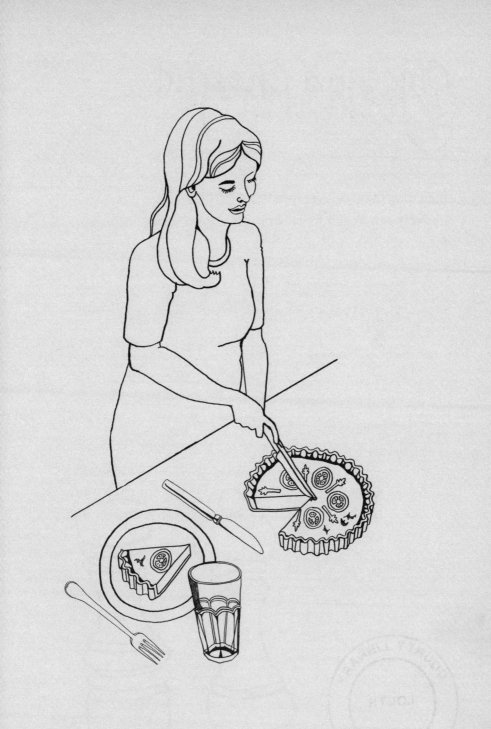

Chic and Cheerful

There comes a time in every woman's life when she starts throwing wine and cream into everything she cooks, usually when she's trying to impress a man. These recipes are a reflection of that adventurous, slightly showing-off phase – but without breaking the bank, putting on weight or, heaven forbid, spending too much time and effort in the kitchen.

Bruschetta

Bruschetta can be a meal by itself when you only want a light lunch or when it's too hot to eat much. If you don't have the time or the inclination for baking your own ciabatta (see page 136), take the easy way out and slice up a loaf or two of fresh French bread instead. As a rough guide, I'd say 1 large ciabatta loaf or French bread stick serves four people.

Serves 4
½lb (225g) mushrooms
butter
1 small bag of spinach
4–6 vine-ripened tomatoes
1 ciabatta loaf or French bread stick
olive oil
black pepper
fresh basil
garlic salt
1oz (25g) Parmesan cheese

1   Preheat the oven to 200c/400f/gas 6. Slice and fry the mushrooms in butter. Wilt the spinach in a small dish with a little water in the microwave or in a pan with a tablespoon of butter. Chop the tomatoes into large chunks.
2   Slice the loaf into six to eight pieces, arrange on a large oven tray and place the bread in the oven for about 5 minutes to crisp it up a bit.
3   Drizzle a little olive oil over each piece of bread and add the toppings.
4   On each piece of bread, put any of the following: chopped tomatoes with black pepper and fresh basil, mushrooms sprinkled with garlic salt or spinach sprinkled with fresh Parmesan.
5   Pour a little melted butter or more olive oil over the bruschetta and put the tray back in the oven for a couple of minutes. Serve hot.

Chicken Terrine

Serve hot or cold with a rice salad. This also makes a delicious
sandwich filling, so try putting thick slices into seedy brown rolls
with raw spinach, tomato and mayonnaise.

> 3–4 chicken fillets (approx 1lb/450g), skin removed
> 8oz (225g) tub of soft cream cheese
> zest and juice of ½ lemon
> 2 tablespoons horseradish (from a jar)
> 2 cloves of garlic
> salt & pepper
> 3 egg whites

1   Preheat the oven to 190C/375F/gas 5.
2   Mince the uncooked chicken in a food processor until the meat
    has been finely chopped without turning to mush. Put the minced
    chicken in a bowl with the cream cheese, lemon zest and juice,
    horseradish, crushed garlic and seasoning.
3   Whisk the egg whites, until stiff and standing up in peaks, in a
    separate bowl.
4   Stir a couple of spoonfuls of egg white into the rest of the
    ingredients, then add all the egg whites and fold in completely.
5   Lightly grease and long-strip-line (see page 13) a standard size
    loaf tin.
6   Put the chicken mixture into the tin, using the spoon to smooth
    it down flat, and cover with a layer of foil, shiny side inwards.
7   Stand the tin in a deep-sided ovenproof dish of water – the water
    should come about two-thirds of the way up the tin – and bake
    for 30 to 40 minutes. Allow the terrine to cool in the tin for about
    5 minutes, then tilt the tin slightly to check that the juice runs
    clear so you know it's cooked through.

Smoked Salmon Cheese

You could make this with soft cream cheese instead of cottage cheese, but the cottage cheese gives it a rougher texture, which I like. Because the fish is blended, you can get away with using cheaper trimmings instead of whole smoked salmon slices. This is perfect with the Rough Oat Biscuits (see page 57) or stirred into warm pasta with a little olive oil as an alternative to pesto.

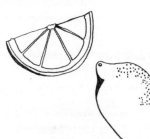

4oz (110g) smoked salmon
8oz (225g) cottage cheese (approx)
2 teaspoons horseradish (from a jar)
a pinch of cayenne pepper
juice of ¼ lemon
a squeeze of lime

1   Cut the smoked salmon into pieces – unless you're using trimmings to start with, in which case you won't need to – and blend in a food processor on the slowest setting for a few seconds to break the salmon up without turning it to mush.
2   Put the salmon in a bowl with the cheese, horseradish, cayenne pepper and lemon and lime juice, according to taste (the amounts listed in the ingredients are just a guide) and mix everything together.
3   Chill in the fridge, in a covered dish or a jar with a lid, for up to four days.

Eggs Mayonnaise Lite

A great housewives' favourite at Tupperware parties in the 1970s. I can't remember the last time I came across eggs mayonnaise on a restaurant menu, but if this simple little starter is also one of your favourites, no matter how embarrassingly uncool and outdated, try making a 'lite' version with the failsafe blender mayonnaise recipe (see Box) mixed with natural yoghurt.

Serves 6
6 large eggs
2 tablespoons mayonnaise (see Box)
4 tablespoons natural yoghurt
salt & pepper
lemon juice
1 round British lettuce
1 small bunch of curly leaf parsley
paprika

1   Bring the eggs to the boil in a small saucepan of cold water and simmer for 10 minutes. Take the pan off the heat and stand the eggs in very cold water for a few minutes. Remove the shells and cut the eggs in half lengthways.

2   In a bowl, beat the mayonnaise and yoghurt together; season with salt, black pepper and lemon juice according to taste.

3   Wash and dry the lettuce and arrange the leaves on six side plates. Put one egg (two halves) in the centre of each and spoon the lite mayonnaise over the top.

4   Garnish with parsley and sprinkle with paprika in the old-fashioned way.

cook's tip

For variation, make spinach mayonnaise. Wilt a handful of fresh spinach in a very little boiling water, drain well, purée the spinach and stir into the mayonnaise at Step 2.

Blender Mayonnaise

The trick is to make the sauce in a food processor with a couple of whole eggs rather than just the yolks, so the whites whisk up and emulsify with the oil more easily, which stops the sauce curdling. This amount of mayonnaise is enough to fill a large jam jar.

> 2 large eggs
> 2 large egg yolks
> 1 teaspoon English mustard
> 2–3 tablespoons white wine vinegar
> salt & pepper
> 1 mug (approx 200ml/7fl oz) olive oil

1. Put the whole eggs and the egg yolks into the blender or food processor with the mustard, vinegar and seasoning and whisk on high speed for a minute.
2. With the blender still on high speed, slowly add the olive oil through the funnel in a thin, steady stream until you have a fairly thick, smooth sauce.
3. Taste the mayonnaise and adjust the seasoning. Transfer to a clean glass jar with a tight-fitting lid and keep in the fridge.

Rainbow Salad

I don't stick to specific recipes for anything very often, so like soups and pasta sauces, my salads never turn out the same way twice, which I imagine is how it is for most people.

Certain fruits go so well with salad vegetables it's a shame not to mix them up on the same plate sometimes, especially in the summer

months, with a complimentary fruit-based dressing and hot, spicy meat from the barbecue.

Anyone who likes sweet-and-sour food will appreciate the contrasting flavours, and it's a bonus that even very young children can be tempted to pick at fruit and vegetables when they look this appealing.

If this is for grown ups, make it yummier still by garnishing platefuls of rainbow salad with edible flowers. Pea flowers, elderflowers, violets, Mexican marigolds, rose geraniums and broad bean flowers are just a few examples of the beautiful varieties available and, although I'm not a great one for kitchen gadgets, I must admit my rainbow salads are more aesthetically pleasing since my mother-in-law gave me a Parisienne cutter for making melon and other soft fruits into balls.

This recipe is really just a starting point for what, after all, is simply an arrangement of summer fruits and veg, cut up and presented prettily on a bed of salad leaves. I like to throw everything together and get as much colour into the mix as I can, but there's no reason why you couldn't arrange the ingredients in shade order or go with a certain theme – say diced cucumber, green pepper and apples (Golden Delicious or Granny Smiths), seedless green grapes and honeydew melon on a bed of watercress – if that's what you prefer. The permutations are endless.

Makes enough for (at least) one very large, family-sized salad

Choose from:
2 wedges of watermelon
2 wedges of honeydew melon
1 nectarine
1 red pepper
1 yellow pepper
½ cucumber
2–3 sticks of celery
1 red apple
1 small bag of baby leaf spinach

1 packet of cherry or baby plum tomatoes
a couple of handfuls of raspberries
a couple of handfuls of purple or green seedless grapes
a handful of fresh mint

1 Peel and trim all fruits and vegetables where necessary. Halve and deseed the melon and chop into small crescents or chunks with the nectarine, or into balls if you have a Parisienne cutter. Dice or slice the peppers, cucumber, celery and apple into roughly same-size pieces, with the skin off or on, according to taste.
2 On a large platter, make a bed of spinach leaves – tear the spinach up a bit if you're not using baby leaf – and arrange all the fruit and vegetables on top, however you like.
3 Garnish with a few sprigs of fresh mint.
4 Sprinkle with a little dressing (see page 24) just before serving with the remainder of the dressing on the side.

For more information about edible flowers and how to order them online, visit www.firstleaf.co.uk. Experiment with a whole variety of very tasty fresh leaves, from peppery baby watercress to super hot rocket.
Visit: www.stevesleaves.co.uk and www.peashoots.com

Dressings

All these dressings are enough for a family-sized salad.

Clementine and Raspberry Yoghurt Dressing

  1 clementine or small sweet orange
  a handful of raspberries
  1 small carton of Greek yoghurt

1 Finely grate the clementine zest into a small bowl and squeeze in
   all the juice. Mix with the raspberries and push everything through
   a fine sieve.
2 Discard the seedy pulp, mix the sieved fruit with the yoghurt
   and serve.

Honey, Lime and Ginger Dressing

  1 lime
  2 tablespoons olive oil
  2 tablespoons sunflower oil
  1 tablespoon runny honey
  fresh ginger, peeled

1 Finely grate the lime zest into a small bowl and squeeze in all
   the juice.
2 Add the oils and honey, mix well, then finely grate some fresh
   ginger into the bowl, according to taste.

Red Wine Dressing

Any soft, fruity red wine will do for this.

> 1 red onion
> 3 cloves of garlic
> ¼ pint (150ml) red wine
> 2 teaspoons lemon juice
> salt & black pepper
> balsamic vinegar

1   Finely chop the onion, crush the garlic and put in a clean jar with the red wine, lemon juice and seasoning. Put the lid on the jar, shake well and leave to stand overnight.
2   Strain the liquid through a fine sieve and add a splash (or two) of balsamic vinegar.
3   Any extra dressing can be kept in the fridge for up to two weeks.

Elderflower Vinaigrette

Elderflower vinaigrette can be made with ready-made elderflower cordial or the homemade version (see page 240).

> 1 tablespoon white wine vinegar
> 2 tablespoons oil (½ pale olive oil, ½ sunflower oil is ideal)
> 2 tablespoons elderflower cordial

1   Mix the vinegar, oils and elderflower cordial together.

Potato Salad

To me, any potato salad is yummy, but the tangy sweetness of
the honey and mustard in this recipe makes it even more so, and
the celery adds freshness and a lovely crunchy texture, which I like.

I haven't given specific quantities for the celery and spring
onions, that's for you to decide. You can also add a handful of cashew
nuts and sultanas.

Feeds 4–6
2lb (900g) new potatoes
½ bunch of spring onions
½ head of celery
zest and juice of ¼ lemon
2 teaspoons wholegrain mustard
1 tablespoon clear honey
1 tablespoon olive oil
2–3 tablespoons Greek yoghurt

1   Cook the potatoes in their skins (peel them or not – I prefer not to)
    until they're just done, then tip them out of the pan on to a large
    tray so they cool down quickly without breaking up. Alternatively,
    you could rinse them in cold water straight away to prevent further
    cooking, but it's better to combine the potatoes with the dressing
    while they're still warm.
2   Top, tail and finely chop the spring onions and celery.
3   Mix the lemon zest and juice, the mustard, honey, olive oil and
    yoghurt in a large bowl. Add the still slightly warm potatoes with
    the vegetables and stir gently.
4   Cover the bowl with a dinner plate and leave to stand at room
    temperature if you plan to eat the potato salad within a few hours.
    Otherwise, keep the potato salad in the fridge until you need it.

Tortilla Shell Salads

Tortilla shells give even the most basic salads the wow factor, but why stick to the most basic when you can do so much more with the minimum amount of effort?

These mini baked tortilla shells taste as good as they look, take only minutes to make and can be served as a first course or a cold buffet dish. Needless to say, the salad suggestions can also be used to fill the full-size Tortilla Baskets (see page 145).

Makes 16 shells
1 packet (8) of flour or corn tortillas
olive oil

Salad suggestions
Shredded iceberg lettuce, diced cucumber and tomato mixed with:
- Bacon, avocado and black olives
- Chicken tikka and crispy fried onions
- Mexican chicken and jalapeños
- Crispy duck in hoisin sauce
- Cottage cheese, smoked salmon and pineapple
- Tuna, prawns and Marie Rose sauce
- Mixed bean salad in mayonnaise

Caesar salad: lettuce, croutons, finely grated Parmesan, yoghurt dressing
Waldorf salad: English lettuce, green apples, celery, walnuts

1   Grease a Yorkshire pudding tin or a very large muffin tin with oil and preheat the oven to 200c/400F/gas 6.
2   Cut the tortillas in half to make 16 semi-circles. Lightly brush both sides with olive oil and twist each semi-circle into a cone. Press firmly into the tins, flattening the tortilla at the base and moulding it around the sides to make a shell or cup. This is easily done when the tortillas are soft and pliable enough to be squeezed into shape, but once they've been baked you can't do much without snapping them.

3   Bake for 5 to 10 minutes until the shells start to brown at the edges and crisp up a bit. Leave the shells to cool on a wire rack, store in an airtight tin and use within two days.

4   Fill the shells with salad, or a combination of salads, and the dressing of your choice:

- Make a homemade version of Marie Rose sauce by mixing 2 teaspoons tomato ketchup and ½ teaspoon paprika with approximately ¼ pint (150ml) mayonnaise.
- For a lemon and mustard mayo, mix 1 teaspoon mustard and lemon juice, according to taste, with approximately 4 tablespoons mayonnaise.
- For cucumber and mint mayonnaise, finely chop ¼ peeled cucumber and a handful of fresh mint and mix with approximately ¼ pint (150ml) mayonnaise and a couple of tablespoons of natural yoghurt.

Roasted Vegetables au Gratin

This could be a side dish or a vegetarian main course with salad and garlic bread.

Serves 4–6
1 large butternut squash
2 red onions
2 peppers (1 red, 1 green)
1lb (450g) button mushrooms
2 teaspoons celery salt
olive oil
½ packet of cream crackers
2oz (50g) Parmesan cheese
2oz (50g) English Stilton

1 Preheat the oven to 200c/400f/gas 6.
2 Cut the butternut squash in half, peel the skin with a potato peeler and remove the pips and the foamy inner bit. Cut the squash into finger-sized sticks.
3 Thinly slice (don't chop) the onions; halve and deseed the peppers; wash the mushrooms and trim the stalks.
4 Put the vegetables into a large ovenproof dish, sprinkle with celery salt and drizzle with a liberal amount of olive oil. Bake for 20 to 25 minutes or until the vegetables are roasted and golden brown.
5 Meanwhile, whiz the cream crackers in a food processor to make fine, white crumbs and mix with the finely grated Parmesan cheese.
6 Take the roasted vegetables out of the oven, crumble the Stilton over the surface and top with the crumb and cheese mixture. Turn the heat up to 220c/425f/gas 7 and return to the oven for another 10 to 15 minutes until the crust is golden.

Tomato Tarte Tatin

A tarte Tatin is usually baked with apples or a combination of apples and another fruit. The tomato version is a savoury flan that makes a perfect light main dish in the summer months, especially with green salad and baby new potatoes.

If you've never cooked a tarte Tatin before you'll be pleased to discover it's a whole lot easier to make than the end result would suggest. Forget the fancy name (I have a French friend who says 'compote of fruit' instead of 'stewed apple') and start thinking of a tarte Tatin as a simple layer of fruit covered in pastry, et voila! That's really all it is.

Serves 4–6
6 deep red (preferably vine-ripened) tomatoes
1oz (25g) butter, plus more for greasing
1 tablespoon honey
2 red onions
fresh basil
1 tablespoon tomato purée
½ teaspoon salt
½lb (225g) ready-made puff pastry

1　Cut the tomatoes into halves. Keep one half for the centre of the pie and cut the rest into quarters. Put the half tomato in the middle of a well-buttered 9 inch (23cm) cake tin, skin side down, and arrange the tomato quarters, also skin side down, however you like.

2　Melt the butter in a frying pan, add the honey and finely chopped onion and cook for a couple of minutes until the onions are golden. Put a handful of fresh torn basil in the pan, followed by the tomato purée and salt. Stir well and cook for another couple of minutes.

3　Meanwhile, on a floured surface, roll out the pastry into a circle slightly larger than the tin.

4   Preheat the oven to 200c/400f/gas 6. Spoon the contents of the pan over the tomatoes, then put the pastry circle over the top and carefully tuck the edges of the pastry around the filling, gently pressing down to make a fairly flat surface.

5   Bake the pie for about 30 minutes until the pastry is risen and golden. At the end of the cooking time, preheat the grill and turn out the pie onto a tray or ovenproof plate. Flash the pie under the grill for a couple of minutes to brown and blister the tomato skins and serve warm.

French Onion Soup

This lovely classic soup is dead easy to make, and made better by
the addition of some very un-classic croutons – see Step 4 or try the
Baked Croutons on page 87. As with all the best recipes, you don't
have to be too precise with the quantities.

Serves 4–6

2lb (900g) onions

1oz (25g) butter

1 tablespoon olive oil

2 teaspoons soft brown sugar

2 cloves of garlic, crushed

1½–2 pints (850ml–1.25 litres) lamb or beef stock

1 very large glass of sherry

4–6 slices of stale bread

1 tablespoon mayonnaise

1oz (25g) Parmesan cheese (approx)

1   Peel and finely slice the onions while you warm the butter and
    olive oil in a very large pan.

2   When the butter has melted, stir in the sugar, then add the onion
    and garlic to the pan. Cook for a few minutes over a medium heat
    until the onion starts browning. Turn the heat down and cook
    without a lid on for another 10 to 15 minutes.

3   Pour the boiling stock into the pan and stir well with a wooden
    spoon, scraping the bottom of the pan to get the caramelised
    brown film mixed into the soup. Add the sherry and gently simmer
    the soup for another 15 to 20 minutes.

4   Once the soup is ready, keep it warm while you cut four circles
    out of each slice of bread with a small pastry cutter. Lightly toast
    the bread circles on one side while you mix the mayonnaise with
    the finely grated Parmesan cheese.

5   Spread the cheesy paste on the un-toasted side of the bread
    and pop back under the grill for another minute or so until

the 'croutons' are crisp and golden.

6 Serve the soup in bowls with three or four croutons floating on the top.

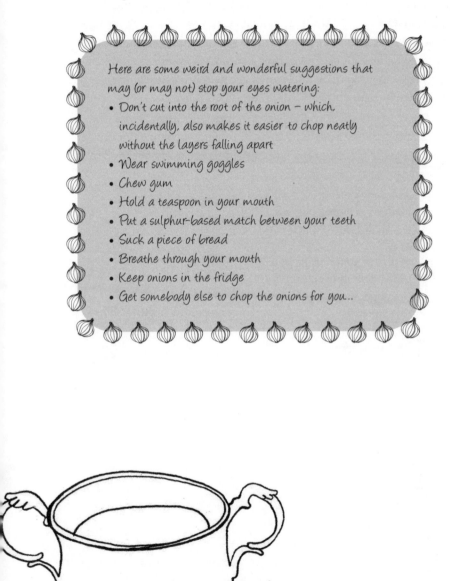

Here are some weird and wonderful suggestions that may (or may not) stop your eyes watering:

- Don't cut into the root of the onion – which, incidentally, also makes it easier to chop neatly without the layers falling apart
- Wear swimming goggles
- Chew gum
- Hold a teaspoon in your mouth
- Put a sulphur-based match between your teeth
- Suck a piece of bread
- Breathe through your mouth
- Keep onions in the fridge
- Get somebody else to chop the onions for you...

Stuffed Spinach Crepes

Because they were one of my children's favourite weekend breakfasts, I used to think of pancakes, or crepes, as a Saturday morning thing (when I was a child we only had them on Shrove Tuesday), but it's a shame to only eat pancakes occasionally when they're as easy as toast and can be made more nutritious and delicious with any number of fillings and sauces.

Purée the spinach in the food processor at Step 2 if you like, but I prefer to tear it up and leave it in pieces so you get a mixture of discernible bits of spinach and plain pancake, as opposed to a completely green pancake.

Makes 6–8 large pancakes
4–5 big tablespoons plain flour
2 eggs
½ pint (275ml) milk (approx)
2 big handfuls of spinach
½ teaspoon nutmeg
salt & pepper

For the stuffing
1 tin of crabmeat
1oz (25g) goats' cheese
1oz (25g) soft cream cheese or Quark
1 small carton of natural yoghurt
2 teaspoons chives

1   Sift the flour into a large bowl and make a well in the centre. Add the beaten egg with about half the milk and beat the mixture with a fork or a small hand whisk, gradually adding the rest of the milk to make a smooth batter.

2   Wilt the spinach by tearing into small pieces and microwaving on full power for about a minute in a covered dish with a tablespoon of water. Alternatively, cook gently in a pan with a tablespoon of butter. Transfer the cooked spinach to the bowl with a slotted

spoon. Add the nutmeg, season with salt and pepper and gently stir the spinach into the batter until well mixed.

3   Pour a cupful of batter into a hot, lightly greased frying pan, tipping the pan as you go to make a pancake.

4   As soon as the surface of the pancake is set, run a blunt knife around the edge and turn it over. Keep the pancakes warm in a very low oven.

5   Drain the tin of crabmeat and mix all the stuffing ingredients together. Spread a spoonful of the mixture in the centre of each pancake. Fold the pancakes into quarters, place on a tray and warm through in the oven on 180c/350f/gas 4 for a few minutes.

> A good way of adding protein to pancakes is to whisk a spoonful of peanut butter into the batter at the end – approximately 1 tablespoon peanut butter for every 1 pint (570ml) of batter. Serve with sliced bananas and golden syrup as a sweet snack or a high-energy breakfast.

Leeks and Mushrooms in Brie Sauce

This can be a side dish with grilled chicken or fish or a vegetarian main course with wild rice and salad.

Serves 4
2–3 leeks
½lb (225g) mushrooms
1 pint (570ml) chicken stock (approx)
1oz (25g) butter or margarine
1 small onion
1oz (25g) plain flour

½ pint (275ml) milk
4oz (110g) Brie
1–2 teaspoons each of dried parsley and chives
salt & pepper

1 Top and tail the leeks, trim the mushroom stalks and thinly slice both vegetables.
2 Put the leeks and mushrooms in a saucepan with just enough chicken stock to cover everything (if you don't have any stock, a teaspoonful of Marmite or Vegemite dissolved in boiling water will do). Cook gently for about 5 minutes until the vegetables are just tender, then drain and keep warm in a shallow ovenproof dish.
3 Meanwhile, melt the butter or margarine in another pan and fry the finely chopped onion until softened, but not browned, then stir in the flour and cook for another minute.
4 Add a little of the milk to the pan, stir well, then gradually add the rest of the milk, stirring or whisking continuously until the sauce thickens.
5 Keep the sauce over a very low heat while you take the rind off the Brie and cut it into small pieces. Add the cheese to the sauce and warm through until the cheese has just about broken down into the sauce. Season with salt and pepper, then pour over the leeks and mushrooms.
6 Sprinkle with parsley and chives and serve immediately.

Have you ever wondered what distinguishes Camembert from Brie? In fact the recipe and production processes are almost identical, except that Brie is made in larger wheels. Camembert's smaller size means the cheese loses moisture and ages more quickly at the ripening stage, which helps to concentrate the flavour.

Grape and Goats' Cheese Flan

If you don't like goats' cheese, try making this with another crumbly white cheese, like Cheshire. This quantity of pastry is just enough to line a 9 inch (23cm) cake or flan tin, so if you want to make a lattice with strips of pastry across the top, use a smaller tin or make the pastry with ½lb (225g) flour and 4oz (110g) of fat.

Being yummy doesn't mean you can't cut corners, so cheat a bit by using ready-to-roll shortcrust pastry, or buy a pre-cooked pastry case and cheat a lot.

Serves 4–6
For the pastry case
6oz (175g) plain flour
3oz (75g) margarine (or 1½ oz each of margarine and lard)
2–3 tablespoons water

For the filling
3 eggs
2 tablespoons natural yoghurt
6oz (175g) goats' cheese
a handful of green seedless grapes

1   Grease a flan tin and preheat the oven to 190C/375F/gas 5.
2   Sift the flour into a mixing bowl, rub in the fat in small pieces until the mixture resembles medium-fine breadcrumbs, then add the water gradually, pinching the mixture together to make a dough. Turn the dough out onto a floured surface and knead for a minute until smooth, then roll out into a circle roughly the same size as the tin.
3   Fit the pastry to the prepared tin (saving the trimmings if you're making a lattice) and put a circle of greaseproof paper on the bottom of the flan, weighing it down with dried beans, peas or pasta. Bake 'blind' for about 15 minutes until the pastry is just golden.

4   Mix the beaten eggs with the yoghurt and grated cheese.
5   Cut the grapes in half and add roughly two-thirds to the egg
    mixture. Scoop the filling into the pastry case, put the rest
    of the grapes on top and press down lightly.
6   Bake for a further 25 minutes until the filling is set firm and
    the pastry is a deep golden brown.
7   Serve warm or cold with salad and more grapes.

Cauliflower Roulade

If you're put off by the rolling process, don't worry. It's nowhere near
as tricky as you might think and if the roulade does crack in places,
you can serve it already cut into slices to disguise the damage. I once
flipped one of these onto a cooling rack as soon as it came out of the
oven and, being still hot, it lost its roundness and went flat. But after
I'd finished cursing it (and myself) I decided I actually preferred this
roulade as a rectangle, so no harm done.

Serves 6
1 small cauliflower
4 eggs
2oz (50g) mature Cheddar cheese
2 tablespoons cottage cheese
2 teaspoons mustard
salt & pepper

For the filling
1oz (25g) butter
2 handfuls of spinach
1 teaspoon nutmeg
1½ tablespoons plain flour
1 small carton of natural yoghurt or 2–3 tablespoons
1oz (25g) mature Cheddar cheese
2 tablespoons cottage cheese
black pepper

1   Line a standard-size rectangular oven tray with greaseproof paper or baking parchment and preheat the oven to 190C/375F/gas 5. Make sure the paper is well greased or oiled so you can peel it off easily once the roulade is cooked.

2   Cut the cauliflower into small pieces including the stalk. Cook in a small saucepan of boiling water or steam for a few minutes until just cooked, but still very firm.

3   Meanwhile, separate the eggs and put the yolks in a bowl with the grated Cheddar, cottage cheese, mustard and seasoning. Put the whites in another bowl.

4   Drain the water from the cooked cauliflower and chop up with a sharp knife and fork. Add the cauliflower to the bowl of egg yolks and cheese and mix well.

5   Whisk the egg whites with a hand-held electric whisk until stiff and standing up in peaks, then fold the whites into the rest of the ingredients. Spread the mixture onto the prepared tray and bake for 20 to 25 minutes until risen and golden.

6   Meanwhile, prepare the filling by melting the butter in a pan, then adding the torn up spinach and nutmeg and cooking gently for a few minutes until the spinach is wilted. Sift in the flour, stirring constantly, and cook for another minute before stirring in the yoghurt. Finally, mix in the cheeses and season with black pepper.

7   When the roulade is cooked, put a layer of greaseproof paper on top of the work surface and turn the roulade out onto the paper. Carefully peel off the paper, wait a minute for the steam to clear, then spread the filling all over the surface.

8   Roll up the roulade by lifting up the short side of the paper nearest to you, gently push the edge over and tightly roll the whole thing up, lifting the paper underneath to help you. Keep the roulade warm in a very low oven until you're ready to serve or leave to cool completely, refrigerate and eat within three days.

Smoked Fish Lasagne

My mother-in-law, Barbara, gave me this recipe, which was made mostly with smoked fish, but even though I've replaced the mackerel with white fish, I'm still calling it smoked fish lasagne, which it will be if you decide to use mackerel or another kind of smoked fish, instead of a white fish like pollock.

Perhaps that's just a clumsy way of saying that these ingredients aren't set in stone, so swap them around to suit yourself. I should also say that the amounts I've given for the cream and Parmesan are conservative estimates – I use quite a bit more of both – so feel free to adjust them if you also tend to be a bit heavy-handed with these things. If you can't get fresh lemon thyme, use dill instead and sprinkle the cooked fish with lots of lemon juice.

Serves 6
2 pints (1.25 litres) milk
2 bay leaves
1 small whole onion, peeled
1½lb (700g) white fish fillets
1 small packet (4oz/110g) cooked and peeled tiger prawns
4 large slices of smoked salmon
2 teaspoons butter
1lb (450g) mushrooms
1 small carton of single cream
1oz (25g) Parmesan cheese
roughly 10–12 sheets of lasagne verde
a big handful of fresh lemon thyme
black pepper

For the sauce
3oz (75g) butter
3 tablespoons plain flour

1   Preheat the oven to 190C/375F/gas 5.
2   Slowly bring 1½ pints (850ml) of the milk to the boil in a very large

pan with the bay leaves and onion, then add the white fish and simmer gently for about 10 minutes.

3   Remove the fish from the pan with a slotted spoon and set it aside with the prawns and the smoked salmon torn into strips. Strain the milk through a sieve into a large jug and add another ½ pint (275ml) of cold milk. Quickly rinse out the pan to make the sauce; no need to wash it properly.

4   Melt the butter in the rinsed out pan, then take the pan off the heat and stir in the flour to make a thick paste. Pour on the milk, stirring all the time. Put the pan back on the heat and stir continuously for a few minutes until you've made a thick, smooth sauce, whisking with a balloon whisk to get rid of any lumps. Sprinkle a couple of tablespoons of cold milk across the surface of the sauce to stop a skin forming.

5   Meanwhile, warm a tablespoon of butter in a frying pan and cut the mushrooms into thick slices. Fry the mushrooms for a couple of minutes until they're just brown, then stir in the cream and about half the Parmesan cheese.

6   Put half the quantities of the fish and prawns at the bottom of a large, deep-sided ovenproof dish, sprinkle with half the lemon thyme, season with black pepper and spoon over roughly a third of the sauce.

7   Cover the fish with a layer of lasagne sheets, followed by all the mushrooms in cream and another layer of lasagne.

8   Put the remainder of the fish, prawns and lemon thyme on top, season and cover with a final layer of lasagne and the rest of the sauce. If the lasagne sheets are poking through the sauce in places, pour on a little boiling water from the kettle. Sprinkle with more Parmesan, cover very loosely with foil and bake for half an hour.

9   Remove the foil and cook for another 20 minutes or so until the sauce on the top is brown and bubbling. Serve with green vegetables or salad.

Fish in Fresh Herbs and Cider

If you make this with plaice or you're cooking for more than four people, you'll need to use two pans, in which case, split the ingredients for the sauce between both lots. You'll find there's more than enough sauce to go round without making more.

Serves 4
4 large white fish fillets
4 tablespoons flour
salt & pepper
1oz (25g) butter
1 handful each of dill and parsley
1 fennel bulb
juice of 1 lemon
½ pint (275ml) dry cider
2–3 tablespoons single cream

1 Dry the fish and sprinkle the flour on a dinner plate. Season with salt and pepper, then coat the fish fillets in the flour on both sides.
2 Melt the butter in a large shallow pan. Wash and roughly chop the dill and parsley and as much of the fennel bulb as you want to use (include some of the fennel frond if you like). Add the herbs and fennel to the warm butter.
3 Put the fish in the pan, skin side up. Fry for about 3 minutes, then turn carefully and fry for another 3 minutes.
4 Squeeze the lemon over the fish and pour the cider into the pan. Cover the pan and simmer gently for about 10 minutes.
5 Put the fish on to plates and spoon as much as you want of the herby cider over, drizzling a little cream down the centre of each one. Serve with new or fried potatoes and green vegetables.

Quenelles in Lemon and Parsley Sauce

Sometimes it's good to be reminded that there is a middle ground with fish, meaning it doesn't have to be steamed and served plain or deep fried in batter and buried under a pile of chips (although I have to admit, that's one of my favourites). These quenelles are very light and low in fat and the sauce won't make much of a dent in your diet if you're trying to lose weight, so you can have them with potatoes as well as a salad and still not worry about the calories.

Serves 4
1lb (450g) white fish
2 egg whites
½ teaspoon nutmeg
½ teaspoon dried coriander leaf
½ teaspoon dried parsley
½ teaspoon onion salt
2 pints (1.25 litres) chicken stock

For the sauce
1 tablespoon margarine
1 tablespoon plain flour
zest and juice of 1 lemon
¼ teaspoon salt
1 level teaspoon sugar

1　Remove the skin from the fish and check for bones, then cut into chunks. Separate the eggs and store the yolks, covered, in the fridge.

2　Put the fish in a food processor and blend on the lowest setting for a few seconds so the fish breaks up without turning completely to mush. Add the egg whites, nutmeg, coriander, parsley and onion salt and process on a higher setting for a few seconds until the mixture becomes a thick paste.

3　Warm the chicken stock in a very large pan while you shape dessertspoonfuls of the paste into quenelles (see Box).

4　Once the stock has boiled, turn it down to a very gentle simmer and poach the quenelles in batches for about 5 minutes, keeping them warm in a low oven once cooked. Skim the stock and take out ½ pint (275ml) to make the sauce.

5　To make the sauce, melt the margarine in a saucepan, then stir in the flour and cook for a minute. Stir in the stock and leave the sauce over a very low heat while you grate the zest and squeeze all the juice from the lemon.

6   Add the lemon zest and juice to the sauce with the salt and sugar. Turn the heat up and stir until the sauce thickens. Pour a little sauce over the quenelles on the plate and serve the rest separately.

Quenelles should be fairly small with pointed ends and look a bit like tulip petals. The right way to shape them is between two dessertspoons, but if you find it easier, use your hands!

Dip the spoons in hot water and scoop a spoonful of the mixture onto one spoon.

Put the empty spoon over the first one and move the spoons in opposite directions to form an oval quenelle.

Use the empty spoon to ease the quenelle off the first spoon and into the stock.

Moules Marinière

'Marinière' means 'sailor style', and the dish Moules Marinière originated in the coastal towns of northern France.

This is an absolute classic – and don't let anyone tell you it's common to serve mussels with chips. If you buy mussels from the fishmonger, you may find they still sell them in pints, so I've given that measurement here too. Vacuum-packed mussels can be found in most supermarkets now, so if you're using these, follow the instructions on the packet. If you're using fresh, put the mussels in a bowl of cold water and thoroughly clean the outer shells with a sharp knife or a nailbrush to remove the beards. Whichever type of mussel you're using, check each one carefully for signs of damage. Discard any with broken shells immediately and once they're cooked, throw away any mussels that haven't opened.

A variation on the traditional recipe uses twice the number of shallots (or even a couple of onions) and lots of herbes de Provence instead of parsley.

Serves 4–6
2oz (50g) butter
4 shallots
2 cloves of garlic
1 small handful of chopped fresh parsley
½ bottle of white wine
3lb (1.35kg) or 3 pints of mussels
2 bay leaves
2 tablespoons crème fraîche

1   Melt the butter in a large, deep pan and fry the chopped shallots, garlic and parsley until the onion is just soft but not coloured.
2   Pour the wine into the pan, add the mussels and bay leaves, cover the pan with a lid and bring to the boil. Simmer gently for about 5 minutes until all the mussels have opened.
3   Set the mussels aside in a bowl and keep warm, then turn the heat up underneath the pan and boil rapidly for a few minutes to reduce the stock slightly.
4   Stir in crème fraîche, whisking with a fork to blend it into the stock.
5   Put the mussels into bowls and pour the sauce over the top. Serve with hot, crisp *pommes frites* and/or crusty bread.

Chicken in Cream Sauce

This lovely little recipe came from an old scrapbook I found in a charity shop. It was unclear whether the chicken was meant to be hot or cold, but I've made it a few times and it's delicious either way, with plain boiled rice and green vegetables or salad.

Serves 4–6
1 whole chicken or 8 large chicken pieces on the bone
2 large egg yolks
2 tablespoons sherry
¼ pint (150ml) single cream
zest and juice of ½ lemon
¼ teaspoon English mustard
salt and white pepper

1 Cook the chicken or chicken pieces in the oven (according to packet instructions) until the meat is tender. If you're using chicken pieces and want to remove the skin first, cover the chicken with a layer of foil to stop the meat drying out.

2 Meanwhile, make the sauce: In a small saucepan, beat the egg yolks, sherry and a tablespoon of the cream over a low heat, gradually adding the rest of the cream and stirring constantly for a couple of minutes until the sauce thickens. Stir the lemon and mustard into the sauce and season with salt and pepper.

3 If you're serving the chicken hot, pour the sauce over the warm chicken as soon as it comes out the oven. To serve cold, allow both chicken and sauce to cool completely before mixing the two together, then cover and refrigerate as soon as possible.

Honey Curry Chicken

This is perfect for those times when you like the idea of a curry, but not the idea of cooking one. Basmati rice would be the obvious thing to go with any curried meat dish, but if a fondness for curry and potatoes is one of *your* guilty pleasures, serve the chicken with paprika potatoes: peel, halve and parboil the potatoes, drain, cut into small chunks, sprinkle with plenty of spice and shallow fry in hot oil. For me, this has the same appeal as chips in curry sauce, but a bit more respectability.

If you have any leftovers, cold honey curry chicken chopped up and mixed with a little dried mint makes a great filler for jacket potatoes.

Serves 4
12 chicken pieces, thighs and drumsticks
flour
salt & pepper
oil
butter
2 teaspoons mild curry powder
2 teaspoons French mustard
4 tablespoons clear honey

1 Remove the chicken skin, wash and dry the meat, then dust in seasoned flour while you warm a couple of tablespoons of oil in a very large pan.
2 Preheat the oven to 190C/375F/gas 5 while you brown the chicken pieces in the hot oil, a few pieces at a time, keeping the meat warm as you go.
3 Add a couple of teaspoons of butter to the pan. Once the melted butter is brown and foaming, add the curry powder, mustard and honey and stir for a minute or so until well blended.
4 Pour the entire contents of the pan over the chicken and bake for 20 to 30 minutes.

Oats and Ends

Why bother baking your own oat bars and biscuits when they're so affordable and available everywhere you look? Well, as always, all I can say is, if it's possible to make something yourself in less time than it takes to run to the supermarket, it's got to be worth having a go at least once.

It's also true that homemade anything is almost always better than shop-bought, which is why eating smaller amounts of biscuits baked by you (or someone else if you're lucky) is infinitely more satisfying than ploughing through half a packet of custard creams. Not only that, if you know any women who have an annoying habit of turning everything to do with food into a healthy eating competition – and let's face it, who doesn't – it's good to be able to put down a plate of homemade biscuits every once in a while and answer the inevitable question with a casual, 'Oh . . . I made them myself.' Ha.

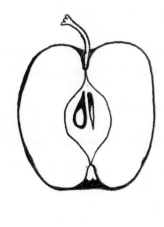

Applejacks

These are the best flapjacks I've ever eaten. Even better than the chocolate-covered ones my daughter makes.

Makes 16 squares
2lb (900g) dessert apples
1–2 tablespoons sugar
4oz (110g) sultanas
1 teaspoon cinnamon
5oz (150g) butter or margarine
4 tablespoons golden syrup
8oz (225g) rolled (porridge) oats
2oz (50g) ground almonds
2 teaspoons icing sugar

1   Lightly grease and long-strip-line a small square tin (see page 13). Preheat the oven to 180c/350f/gas 4.
2   Peel and core the apples, slice thinly and put in a saucepan with the sugar and a very little water (just enough to stop the fruit sticking to the bottom of the pan). Simmer gently for about 15 minutes until the fruit is soft, then take the pan off the heat.
3   Meanwhile, wash the sultanas in warm water and put them in the pan with the stewed apples. Add the cinnamon and stir into the fruit.
4   Melt the butter and golden syrup in another saucepan, then stir in the oats and ground almonds. If the mixture is still too loose and wet, just add more porridge oats until it looks right to you.
5   Put three-quarters of the oat mixture into the prepared tin and press down to make an even layer. Cover with the fruit, then top the fruit with the remainder of the oat mixture. Bake for about 30 minutes until the top is firm and slightly golden.
6   Let the flapjacks cool in the tin. After about 20 minutes, mark into squares and leave to cool completely. Dust the flapjacks with icing sugar, cut and keep in an airtight tin.

Treacle Flapjacks

Black treacle is a good source of iron and adds a bit of extra depth and sweetness to this basic flapjack recipe.

Makes 16 squares
4 tablespoons honey
2 tablespoons black treacle
6oz (175g) butter
12oz (350g) rolled (porridge) oats
2oz (50g) dried apricots
2oz (50g) sultanas
1oz (25g) flax seeds

1 Lightly grease and long-strip-line a small tin, approx 8 inches (20cm) square (see page 13). Preheat the oven to 170C/325F/gas 3.
2 Put the honey, treacle and butter in a large saucepan over a low heat until the butter has melted completely, then add the oats, chopped dried fruit and seeds and mix well.
3 Press the mixture into the prepared tin, smoothing it down evenly with the back of a spoon. Bake for 20 to 30 minutes until the surface is firm and golden. Leave to cool in the tin and mark into squares.
4 When the flapjacks are completely cold, cut them up and store in an airtight tin for up to one week.

cook's tip

Instead of fruit, add desiccated coconut and chocolate chips to the flapjacks or cover the cooked flapjacks with a thin layer of chocolate in the tin and cut them up when the chocolate sets.

Digestive Biscuits

I'm a great fan of shop-bought digestives, but these are nice too, and, it goes without saying, additive-free. It also goes without saying that you can make chocolate digestives simply by leaving out the dusting of oat bran at the end and spreading a thin layer of melted chocolate, milk or plain, across the surface of each one. Allow the chocolate to dry completely before putting the biscuits in a tin.

Makes 24–30 biscuits
6oz (175g) wholemeal flour
2oz (50g) fine oatmeal or oat bran, plus more for dusting
1 teaspoon baking powder
½ teaspoon salt
3oz (75g) margarine
3oz (75g) muscovado (or other dark brown) sugar
3 tablespoons milk
3 tablespoons water

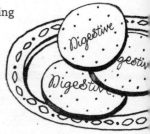

1 Preheat the oven to 190C/375F/gas 5 and lightly grease two baking trays.
2 Sift the flour, oatmeal or oat bran, baking powder and salt into a mixing bowl. Add the margarine in small pieces and rub in with your fingertips until the mixture resembles medium-fine breadcrumbs.
3 Stir in the sugar, breaking up any little lumps with your fingers.
4 Add the milk to the bowl and pinch the mixture together with your hand to make a firm dough.
5 On a floured surface, roll out the dough to a biscuit thickness (whatever looks right to you) and use a pastry cutter or cup to cut the dough into rounds, re-rolling the trimmings as you go.
6 Place the biscuits on the greased baking trays. Brush with a very little water and sprinkle with a light dusting of oatmeal or oat bran to finish.
7 Bake for 10 to 12 minutes until crisp and just golden.

Granola

It's hard to say exactly how many portions these quantities make, but as a rough guide, I'd say about a dozen loose servings of granola or sixteen granola bars (see page 53). Double it up if you want more and add extra fruit, seeds and coconut according to your own taste.

Seeds have been one of my good habits since the days when sitting my children in front of the TV with a bowl of pumpkin or sunflower seeds guaranteed me half an hour of peace. They used to love splitting them open with their teeth and picking the seeds out of the shells. These days, I take the easy way out and buy pouches of Linwoods seeds; flax seeds, mixed seeds and hemp. They're already shelled and ready to be sprinkled over porridge or mixed with everything from breadcrumbs to crumble toppings (sweet and savoury), which makes them perfect for boosting the nutritional value of a meal without compromising the taste or texture.

Makes about 16 servings
1–1½ tablespoons sunflower oil
½lb (225g) rolled (porridge) oats
4oz (110g) nuts (hazelnuts, almonds, walnuts or a mixture of these)
2oz (50g) desiccated coconut
2oz (50g) flax seed mix (any variety)
6 tablespoons honey
4oz (110g) dried apricots
4oz (110g) dried cranberries

1 Warm the oil in a large deep-sided ovenproof dish in an oven preheated to 180C/350F/gas 4.
2 Mix all the ingredients together except for the fruit and honey. Spread them across the ovenproof dish and bake for about 20 minutes, taking the dish out of the oven and giving it a good shake every few minutes.
3 Empty the cooked granola into a large bowl and, while it's still warm, trickle the honey over everything and stir well.
4 As soon as the granola is completely cold, add the chopped dried fruit, mix well again and store in an airtight tin or large jar for up to 2 weeks.

Granola Bars

Makes 16 bars
4oz (110g) butter
4oz (110g) golden or maple syrup
½lb (225g) rolled (porridge) oats
4oz (110g) dried apricots
4oz (110g) dried cranberries
4oz (110g) nuts (hazelnuts, almonds, walnuts or a mixture of these)
2oz (50g) desiccated coconut
2oz (50g) flax seed mix (any variety)

1 Lightly grease and long-strip-line a small 8 × 10 inch (20 × 25cm) rectangular tin (see page 13). Preheat the oven to 170C/325F/gas 3.
2 Warm the butter and syrup in a large saucepan over a low heat, stirring occasionally until the butter has melted.
3 Add the rest of the ingredients to the pan and mix well, then press the mixture into the prepared tin, smoothing it out with the back of a spoon. Bake for about 30 minutes until the surface is just golden.
4 Leave to cool in the tin and mark into squares. Remove the granola bars from the tin when cold and store in an airtight tin.

Sweet Malted Oat Cakes

Almost unbelievably, these are even quicker and easier to make than flapjacks.

Makes about 20 cakes
½lb (225g) rolled (porridge) oats
2 tablespoons soft brown sugar
3 tablespoons or 1 × 32g sachet Horlicks
4 tablespoons sunflower oil
4 tablespoons milk

1   Lightly grease and long-strip-line a small 8 × 10 inch (20 × 25cm) rectangular tin (see page 13). Preheat the oven to 170C/325F/gas 3.
2   Put the dry ingredients into a mixing bowl, mix everything together; add the oil and milk and stir well. (Add a drop more milk if the mixture seems a bit dry.)
3   Press the mixture into the prepared tin and bake for 20 to 30 minutes until the surface is firm and golden. Leave to cool in the tin and mark into squares.
4   Remove from the tin when cold and store in an airtight tin for up to a few days.

Fig Rolls

A homemade fig roll is not necessarily a thing of beauty, but the taste and texture more than make up for that. Figs are rich in nutrients, and even in biscuit form, at around 60 calories a pop, they're a healthier sweet snack than a handful of chocolate fingers.

Makes about 16
½lb (225g) plain flour
5oz (150g) butter or margarine

2oz (50g) soft brown sugar
1 large egg yolk
2 teaspoons milk, plus more for glazing
½lb (225g) dried ready-to-eat figs
1 tablespoons honey

1   Sift the flour into a large mixing bowl. Add the fat in small pieces and rub in with your fingertips until the mixture resembles medium-fine breadcrumbs. Stir in the sugar and make a well in the centre.

2   Mix the beaten egg yolk in a cup with the milk. Add to the flour and pinch the mixture together with your hands to form a fairly soft dough. Wrap the dough in clingfilm or foil and chill in the fridge for half an hour.

3   Meanwhile, put the figs in a small saucepan with a very little hot water (barely enough to cover) and simmer gently for a few minutes until the fruit is slightly swollen. Strain the fruit and mash it up very thoroughly with a sharp knife and fork before mixing with the honey.

4   Preheat the oven to 180C/350F/gas 4 and lightly grease two baking trays.

5   On a floured surface, roll out the dough to a large rectangle, trim the edges and cut the rectangle in half to make two strips, roughly 3½ inches (9cm) wide.

6   Spread the figs down the centre of each strip, then fold the pastry over the fruit on either side, sealing the join with a little milk.

7   Cut the rectangles into small rolls about 1½ inches (4cm) wide (or whatever looks right to you), then place them on the baking trays, join side down, and brush with more milk. Bake for about 10 to 15 minutes until the pastry is just golden.

Lemon and Almond Biscuits

Biscuits made from rice flour are lighter and whiter than biscuits made with wheat and have a lovely crumbly texture. Make these biscuits into snaps or 'thins' (hard and crisp instead of soft and crumbly) by leaving out the egg and adding a bit more lemon juice.

Makes at least 36 biscuits
zest and juice of 1 lemon
4oz (110g) butter or margarine
4oz (110g) caster sugar, plus extra for dusting
8oz (225g) rice flour
4oz (110g) ground almonds
1 egg

1   Put the finely grated rind of the lemon and all the juice into a large mixing bowl with the butter or margarine and sugar. Beat with a hand-held electric whisk until the mixture is pale and fluffy.
2   Add the sifted rice flour and ground almonds to the bowl and beat for another minute or so with the whisk on the slowest setting until all the ingredients are combined.
3   Add the beaten egg to the mixture a little at a time (you may not need it all) to make a soft dough, then wrap and refrigerate the dough for about half an hour.
4   Preheat the oven to 180c/350f/gas 4 and lightly grease two large baking trays.
5   Roll out the dough on a lightly floured surface and cut into rounds. Place the biscuits on the prepared trays, prick with a fork and sprinkle a bit more caster sugar over the top.
6   Bake for 10 to 15 minutes until the biscuits are firm and slightly golden.

Rough Oat Biscuits

Real rough oat biscuits are made purely with oats. I like these better because I think the addition of wholemeal flour makes the dough easier to handle and improves the texture of the finished biscuits.

Makes at least 24 biscuits
1oz (25g) margarine
4oz (110g) oatmeal or oat bran, plus extra for dusting
2oz (50g) wholemeal flour
½ teaspoon salt
a pinch of bicarbonate of soda

1   Lightly oil two large baking trays. Preheat the oven to 150C/300F/gas 2.
2   Pour 4fl oz (120ml) warm, previously boiled, water into a large, heatproof mixing bowl.
3   Add the margarine to the water and, when melted, add the oatmeal or oat bran, flour, salt and bicarbonate of soda to the bowl and use a wooden spoon to mix to a firm dough.
4   Roll out the dough as thin as you can on a floured surface and cut out rounds with a cup or pastry cutter, re-rolling the trimmings as you go.
5   Put the biscuits on the baking trays and dust with a little more oatmeal. Bake for about 45 minutes until firm. Allow the biscuits to cool completely on a wire rack and store in an airtight tin for up to two weeks.

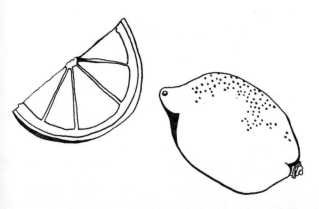

Cheese Biscuits

A bit less worthy than rough oat cakes, but still more wholesome than cream crackers, and perfect with soft cheeses and fruit.

Makes 24 (approx)
6oz (175g) wholemeal flour
2oz (50g) oatmeal or oat bran
1 teaspoon baking powder
½ teaspoon salt
4oz (110g) margarine
2oz (50g) Cheddar cheese
2oz (50g) sesame seeds
4 tablespoons milk

1   Put the flour, oatmeal or bran, baking powder and salt in a large mixing bowl. Add the margarine in small pieces and rub in until the mixture resembles medium-fine breadcrumbs.
2   Mix in the grated cheese and sesame seeds.
3   Add the milk, a little at a time, and pinch the mixture together with your hands to make a fairly soft, smooth dough.
4   Knead the dough on a floured surface for a minute, then wrap and refrigerate for about half an hour.
5   Preheat the oven to 190C/375F/gas 5. Roll out the dough on the floured surface to about 3mm and cut into rounds. Bake for 10 to 15 minutes until golden.

Just Dessert

For me, cakes, puddings and afters – or whatever you want to call them – are the true definition of 'yummy'. No further explanations or excuses are needed, as long as you've eaten your greens first.

Baileys Cream Pie

I've included a chocolate cake recipe (see Box) for anyone who wants
to make the dessert from scratch, but a shop-bought Jamaican ginger
cake or rich chocolate sponge is perfect for this (the stickier the
better) and cuts the preparation time down to a matter of minutes.
I make my pie in an 8–9 inch (20–23cm) non-stick pie dish, but if you
don't have one, a cake tin will do.

To make your own Irish cream liqueur, see page 235 and, for the
record, 3fl oz (75ml) fills a liqueur glass to the brim, so if you have
liqueur glasses at home, use one to measure the Baileys.

> 12oz (350g) ginger or chocolate cake (see Box)
> 1oz (25g) butter
> 2 tablespoons golden syrup
> 11oz (300g) tub of soft cream cheese
> 3fl oz (75ml) Baileys, plus more for pouring
> 11fl oz (325ml) carton of whipping cream
> 1 tablespoon sugar
> ½oz (10g) chocolate, milk or plain

1   To make the base for the cream pie, break the cake up into chunks
    and whiz in a blender or food processor for a minute to turn it into
    crumbs. Meanwhile, put the butter and golden syrup in a small
    saucepan and heat gently until the butter has melted.
2   Lightly grease an 8–9 inch (20–23cm) non-stick pie dish or cake tin.
3   Thoroughly mix the melted butter and syrup into the cake crumbs
    and use the back of a spoon to press the mixture into the prepared
    tin in a firm, even layer. Cover with clingfilm and leave to chill in
    the fridge.
4   To make the cream filling, beat the cream cheese with a wooden
    spoon until smooth, add the Baileys and stir until well blended.
5   In a separate bowl, beat the whipping cream and sugar with a
    hand-held electric whisk to the point where it's very thick and
    looks slightly holey.

6 Carefully fold the sweet whipped cream into the cream cheese and Baileys, then spoon the mixture onto the base, piling it high in the middle and using the back of the spoon to swirl it. Cover loosely with clingfilm and chill in the fridge for at least 4 hours.

7 Grate the chocolate all over the top before serving and pour a spoonful (or two) of Baileys over the pie on the plate.

A homemade chocolate sponge

6oz (175g) butter
6oz (175g) dark brown sugar
3 eggs
6oz (175g) self-raising flour
2oz (50g) cocoa powder
2 teaspoons instant coffee
1 tablespoon golden syrup

Grease and base-line two 8 inch (20cm) sandwich tins and preheat the oven to 190C/375F/gas 5. Cream the butter and sugar until pale and fluffy, then gradually add the beaten eggs, whisking continuously. Fold in the sifted flour and cocoa powder with a large metal spoon. Mix the coffee dissolved in 2 tablespoons boiling water and the golden syrup together in a mug; stir into the cake mixture, divide the mixture between the prepared tins and bake for 25 to 30 minutes.

Cherry and Chicory Pie

There's a cooking cherry tree at the bottom of our garden that yields a mass of fruit every summer, but because the cherries don't ripen simultaneously, there only seems to be a period of about two days when there's enough bright red fruit to make the picking worthwhile. After that the birds strip the branches completely, so most years I half-heartedly pick the fruit in fits and starts, then end up throwing it all back to the birds when it's finally gone off in the fruit bowl.

Anyway, I do occasionally manage to pull myself together in time to pick enough fruit for a pie or two, but I would never have thought of mixing the cherries with chicory until I ate a gorgeous plum tart with chicory made by Rose Prince, the cookery writer, which was delicious and had quite a different flavour from any fruit pie I've ever tasted. That was the inspiration for this recipe.

1lb (450g) cherries
2 tablespoons white breadcrumbs
1 head of chicory
2 tablespoons ground almonds
2 tablespoons sherry
2 tablespoons sugar (soft brown or caster)
2 teaspoons cinnamon
¾lb (350g) pastry (approx) (see Box)
3 tablespoons milk (approx)

1   Remove the cherry stones by peeling the flesh away with a small sharp knife and squeezing out the stone. Don't worry about trying to preserve the shape of the fruit, it doesn't matter for this recipe.
2   Toast the breadcrumbs by spreading them out on a large oven tray and putting them under the grill or in the oven for about 5 minutes. They should be a deep golden brown, but not burnt.
3   Top and tail the chicory, slice thinly and put in a bowl with the cherries, ground almonds, toasted breadcrumbs, sherry, sugar and cinnamon, stirring well.

4   Meanwhile, make the pastry and rest the dough in the fridge for about half an hour.

5   Lightly grease an 8 inch (20cm) pie dish and roll out and cut the pastry to fit, using roughly two-thirds for the pie and the remaining third for the lid. Preheat the oven to 190C/375F/gas 5.

6   Prick the base of the pie with a fork a few times, then fill with the cherry and chicory mixture. Wet the outer rim of the pastry with a little milk, cover the pie with the lid and pinch the edges together between your thumb and forefinger to make a thick crust.

7   Glaze the top with more milk and use the pastry trimmings to make leaves for decorating the lid of the pie. Bake for about 45 minutes until the pastry is golden.

cook's tip

I like the orange pastry on page 152, but make it with sweet or shortcrust pastry if you prefer. If you want the pie but not the hassle of pastry, put the cherry and chicory mixture into a ready-made pastry case – or straight into a buttered ovenproof dish – and cover the fruit with a sweet crumble topping (see page 67).

Marbled Meringues

For me, meringue is the next yummiest sweet thing after chocolate, and contrary to what you may think, most meringue recipes are very simple and so delicious that the end result always justifies the means (even if you hate waiting for the meringue to dry out agonisingly slowly in the oven).

The worst meringue I've ever (not) eaten came from one of those pavement cafés that always has beautiful marbled meringues in the window, and even though I knew it wouldn't taste anywhere near as good as it looked, I still couldn't believe how dreadful it actually was. Only the mushy, uncooked egg white inside convinced me that the meringue was edible at all (for want of a better word) because the crisp outer shell tasted weirdly of nothing and the texture was so artificial, when I put the first forkful into my mouth I thought they'd given me a plaster display model by mistake.

Anyway, there's no point to this story, other than to say that less outwardly perfect homemade meringues taste better than they look, and the only slightly tricky part is gauging how long to leave them in the oven so they cook through without browning. If you're not sure, bake them at the lowest temperature for a slightly longer time, rather than overcook them. Some meringues look better with a bit of colour, but these should be a brilliant white.

For best results, use a natural fruit sauce (Hartley's do good ones in squeezy bottles) and steer clear of the cheaper, synthetic ice cream syrups. Icing sugar is best for this recipe, use salt if you don't have cream of tartar and, finally, although I always keep eggs at room temperature, ideally the egg whites should be chilled, so if you can, put the eggs in the fridge the night before.

Makes 6 meringues
2 egg whites
1 big pinch of cream of tartar
6oz (175g) icing sugar
strawberry ice cream sauce

1   Switch the oven on to the lowest setting and line a baking tray with very lightly oiled baking parchment or greaseproof paper.
2   Put the egg whites in a very clean mixing bowl with the cream of tartar (or salt) and beat with a hand-held electric whisk on the highest setting until stiff enough to stand up in peaks.
3   Sift in half the icing sugar and whisk on high again, then fold in the remainder of the sugar with a metal spoon.
4   Swirl the ice cream syrup over the meringue, holding the bottle

high over the bowl, then stir gently *once or twice only* to get a
marbled effect.

5   Scoop a large spoonful of meringue onto the prepared tray, easing
    it off the spoon slowly to give the meringue height and a good
    shape. Use the spoon or a fork to improve the shape of the
    meringues on the tray at the end, but keep the handling to
    an absolute minimum and don't mess with them too much.

6   Leave the meringues to dry out in the oven on the lowest setting –
    or slightly higher, depending how hot your oven is – for between
    2 and 3 hours.

7   Allow the meringues to cool and harden completely at room
    temperature for at least 2 more hours and store in an airtight tin
    for up to two weeks.

Mango and Pomegranate Pavlova

Sometimes the prohibitive cost of pomegranates almost stops me
buying them, so I try and think of a pomegranate as an affordable
treat, rather than a ridiculously expensive fruit with ideas above its
station. It may be six times the price of an apple, but it's still cheaper
and infinitely better for you than a Terry's Chocolate Orange, which,
funnily enough, is another one of those things where the ritual
involved in the eating is part of the fun – for some people.

I haven't got the patience to deseed a pomegranate myself very
often. If I turn it upside down and bash it with a wooden spoon like
Nigella, I always end up with purple juice and pomegranate seeds
splattered all over the worktop, and I can never separate the seeds
from the shell without getting most of the pith too, so I usually just
cut the fruit in half and get my daughter to do the 'fun' bit for me.

This is another easy meringue recipe and it's easier still if you
cheat with shop-bought meringues instead of making your own.
That way you can choose either to make the dessert with one large
meringue, as it is here, or break up several smaller meringue nests

into rough pieces to mix with the fruit and cream before piling the whole lot onto a plate. Alternatively, use the smallest ready-made pink and white meringues (in which case, leave them whole) and finish with a sprinkling of tiny silver balls for added kitsch.

4oz (110g) caster sugar, plus a couple more teaspoons
4 egg whites
1 mango
1 pomegranate
1 small carton of double cream
a few drops of peppermint essence
a few sprigs of fresh mint

1   Put the sugar in a small saucepan with 2 tablespoons water, bring to the boil very gently over a low heat until the sugar has dissolved completely. Remove the syrup from the heat and set aside.
2   Meanwhile, use a marker pen or felt tip to draw a large circle around a 9 inch (23cm) cake tin on a sheet of greaseproof paper. Place the sheet on a baking tray with the pen side down so you can see the outline clearly through the paper without the ink coming into contact with the food. Preheat your oven to its lowest setting.
3   Whisk the egg whites until stiff and standing up in peaks, then pour the syrup onto the meringue very slowly in a thin, steady trickle, whisking continuously.
4   Spoon the meringue onto the baking tray inside the circle and use the spoon and a fork to hollow the meringue out in the middle to make a kind of nest. Bake for 1½ to 2 hours until the meringue is crisp and firm on the outside.
5   Once the meringue has cooled completely – give it at least 1 hour – peel and chop the mango and scoop out the pomegranate seeds with a dessertspoon. Whisk the double cream with a few drops of peppermint essence and a couple of teaspoons of sugar.
6   Put the meringue nest on a large plate, fill with cream and top with the fruit. Garnish with a few sprigs of fresh mint and keep in the fridge for up to two days. As if.

Raspberry, Rhubarb and Apple Crumble

I made this once when everyone wanted a pudding and all I could find, apart from the usual store cupboard ingredients, was leftover bits and pieces from one of my daughter's cake-making sessions, rhubarb from my brother's allotment, half a packet of raspberries and two cooking apples slightly past their best in the fruit bowl. But that's the beauty of crumbles. Apart from being one of the easiest, most foolproof and failsafe recipes ever, you can make them with whatever odds and ends you have handy and the result still looks and tastes as good as any dessert that would have taken twice as much time and trouble.

A crumble mixture is one of the most versatile toppings for a variety of dishes. Leave out the sugar and add a couple of tablespoons of grated Cheddar cheese to the mix for meaty crumbles, roughly the same quantity of crushed up Crunchy Nut Cornflakes for fruit crumbles, and porridge oats to both sweet and savoury crumbles.

Makes enough for 4–6
1lb (450g) rhubarb (approx)
2 cooking apples
2 tablespoons sugar
4oz (110g) raspberries

For the crumble
6 tablespoons plain flour
3oz (75g) butter of margarine
1 tablespoon sugar
½ packet mini marshmallows
2 tablespoons desiccated coconut

1   Top and tail the rhubarb and cut into chunks. Peel and core the apples and cut into chunks roughly the same size as the rhubarb.

2   Put the rhubarb and apple in a saucepan with the sugar (use more than 2 tablespoons if you like) and a very little water and simmer over a low heat for about 15 minutes until the fruit has softened and the liquid is syrupy.

3   Make the crumble by sifting the flour into a mixing bowl and rubbing in the butter or margarine until the mixture resembles medium-fine breadcrumbs. Stir in the sugar, mini marshmallows and coconut.

4   Wash the raspberries, mix with cooked fruit and put the whole lot in a deep-sided casserole dish.

5   Cover with the crumble topping and cook on 170–180c/325–350F/gas 3–4 for 20 to 30 minutes until the top is firm and golden. Serve with custard or cream.

Very Berry Meringue Cake

This is the fruit version of the chocolate Flake Cake on page 195. Don't be put off by the slightly long list of ingredients or the number of stages; this is basically just a plain Victoria sponge cake where you whisk the egg whites separately to make an extra layer. Unless you drop the cake when you're taking it out of the oven, you're guaranteed a great result with this recipe every time. In fact, it's so stunningly simple and effective, if I was mad enough to go on *Come Dine With Me*, I'd do this for dessert. It really is that good.

4 eggs
½ teaspoon salt
4 tablespoons milk (approx 50ml)
2 teaspoons vanilla essence
2oz (50g) margarine
6oz (175g) caster sugar
4oz (110g) self-raising flour

To decorate
¼lb (110g) frozen mixed berries
2 tablespoons flaked almonds
1 small carton of double or whipping cream

1   Lightly grease and base-line two 7–8 inch (18–20cm) springform
    or sandwich tins. Preheat the oven to its lowest setting and leave
    the frozen fruit at room temperature to defrost (which should only
    take a couple of hours).
2   Separate the eggs. Put the whites in one mixing bowl with the salt.
    Put the egg yolks in a small bowl or measuring jug with the milk
    and vanilla essence.
3   For the sponge, put the margarine and 2oz (50g) of the sugar
    in another mixing bowl and cream together with a hand-held
    electric whisk until light and fluffy. Add the egg yolks, a little at
    a time, beating continuously.
4   Sift the flour into the bowl and fold it in with a large metal spoon.
    Add a little more milk if you need to, to get a soft dropping
    consistency.
5   Divide the mixture equally between the two prepared cake tins
    as evenly as you can and quickly wash and dry the whisk blades.
6   Whisk the egg whites until stiff enough to stand up in peaks, then
    add half the remaining 4oz (110g) sugar at a time, whisking after
    each addition until all the sugar is incorporated and the meringue
    is as stiff as it needs to be, i.e. if you turn the bowl upside down,
    it won't fall out.
7   Spoon a layer of meringue over the sponge mixtures and use
    the back of the spoon to flatten it out, finishing with a swirl
    and sprinkling a handful of almonds on top of each one.
8   Bake for 30 to 40 minutes until the meringue is firm on top
    and a very light pinkish beige in colour, then let the cakes cool
    completely before taking them out of the tin. To do this, run a
    blunt knife around the edge, then release the spring, remove
    the outside of the tin carefully, turn the cakes over and peel away
    the greaseproof paper. If it's a sandwich tin, place a dinner plate

over the top, carefully turn it over, ease the tin away from the cake, put another plate over the top of the cake – which is actually the bottom – and turn it the right way up.

9   Whisk the cream till thick, then cover one of the cakes with the cream and fruit, saving the best looking cake to be the top layer, and sandwich the two halves together. Keep in the fridge and eat within three days.

Sugar and Cinnamon Fruit Buns

These buns are lovely, but they only stay fresh for a day or two at the most. After that, they're better toasted. If you don't have cube sugar, use granulated.

Makes 6 buns
2–3 tablespoons milk
1 sachet of dried yeast
½lb (225g) strong white bread flour
1oz (25g) butter
1 tablespoon caster sugar
1 egg
2oz (50g) dried mixed fruit
1 teaspoon ground cinnamon
a small handful (1oz/25g) of cube sugar

1   Warm the milk in the microwave or in a small pan for a very few seconds until it's just tepid, then sprinkle the dried yeast over the surface and leave to stand at room temperature for about 15 minutes.

2   Sift the flour into a large mixing bowl, add the butter in small pieces and rub in with your fingertips until the mixture resembles medium-fine breadcrumbs.

3   Add the sugar to the mixture and make a well in the centre. Pour the milk, yeast and the beaten egg into the well and mix

to a fairly smooth dough with your hands.

4   Knead the dough on a floured surface for 10 minutes, then put it
    into a lightly greased bowl or on a very large oven tray lined with
    clingfilm. Cover with a damp cloth and prove the dough in a warm
    place for one hour.

5   Meanwhile, mix the dried fruit with the cinnamon and grease
    a loose-bottomed 6–7 inch (15–18cm) cake tin.

6   When the dough has doubled in size, knock it back and knead
    it again for a few more minutes. Flatten it out into a large circle,
    cover with the fruit and roll the dough back into a ball, kneading
    it just enough to get all the fruit incorporated into the dough.

7   Tear the dough into six same-sized pieces and roll each piece
    into a ball. Arrange them in the cake tin with one in the middle
    surrounded by the other five so the sides are just touching. Prove
    a second time until the dough has doubled in size again.

8   About 10 minutes before the end of the proving time, preheat the
    oven to 190C/375F/gas 5 and crush up the sugar cubes. Put half
    to one side and the other half in a small saucepan with a couple
    of tablespoons of water. Put the pan over a very low heat until all
    the sugar has dissolved, stirring occasionally, then turn the heat
    up a bit and simmer for a few minutes to make a thin syrup.

9   Brush the buns with a liberal amount of syrup – you may not need
    to use it all – and sprinkle the rest of the sugar crystals all over the
    surface.

10 Bake for about 30 minutes until the buns are a deep golden brown.
    Allow the bun ring to cool for a while before taking it out of the
    tin in one piece and leaving it on a wire rack to cool completely.
    Store in an airtight tin and eat within one week.

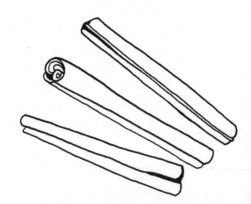

Iced Buns

These are the sugar and cinnamon fruit buns without the cinnamon and fruit to give them a veneer of respectability. Even worse (or better) they're covered in a layer of sticky pink or white icing, so you can't leave them hanging around for a few days before toasting them, they need to eaten on the same day. Oh no.

Makes 6 buns
2–3 tablespoons milk
1 sachet of dried yeast
½lb (225g) strong white bread flour
1oz (25g) butter
1 tablespoon caster sugar
1 egg
3–4 heaped tablespoons icing sugar
pink food colouring

1   Warm the milk in the microwave or in a small pan for a few seconds until it's just tepid, then sprinkle the dried yeast over the surface and leave to stand at room temperature for about 15 minutes.
2   Sift the flour into a large mixing bowl, add the butter in small pieces and rub in with your fingertips until the mixture resembles medium-fine breadcrumbs.
3   Add the sugar to the mixture and make a well in the centre. Pour the milk, yeast and the beaten egg into the well and mix to a fairly smooth dough with your hands.
4   Knead the dough on a floured surface for 10 minutes, then put it into a lightly greased bowl or on a very large oven tray lined with clingfilm. Cover with a damp cloth and prove the dough in a warm place for one hour.
5   Meanwhile, grease a loose-bottomed 6–7 inch (15–18cm) cake tin.
6   When the dough has doubled in size, knock it back and knead again for a few more minutes, then tear into six same-sized pieces.

Roll each piece into a ball and arrange them in the cake tin with one in the middle surrounded by the other five so the sides are just touching. Prove a second time until the dough has doubled in size again.

7   Preheat the oven to 190C/375F/gas 5.

8   Bake the buns for about 30 minutes until they are a deep golden brown. Allow the bun ring to cool for a while before taking it out of the tin in one piece and leaving it on a wire rack to cool completely.

9   Sift the icing sugar into a mixing bowl (with a very few drops of food colouring if you want pink icing) and stir in a few table-spoonfuls of cold water, a little at a time, until the icing is the consistency you want.

10 Cover the buns with a thick layer of icing, using a knife dipped in hot water to help spread the icing all over the surfaces. Best eaten on the day (see above).

Lemon Drizzle Cake

This is a classic and as easy as falling off a log. I make lemon drizzle cake with an all-in-one method, which is even quicker and easier than a regular quick and easy sponge cake recipe. In fact, it could almost be slummy . . . (see also the Tray Bake Cake on page 110).

For the cake
½lb (225g) self-raising flour
1 teaspoon baking powder
½lb (225g) caster sugar
½lb (225g) butter or margarine
4 eggs
zest and juice of 1 lemon

For the drizzle
zest and juice of ½ lemon
1½–2 tablespoons icing sugar

1 Lightly grease and base-line a 9 inch (23cm) cake tin and preheat the oven to 170c/325F/gas 3.
2 Sift the flour and baking powder into a large mixing bowl and make a deep well in the centre. Put the sugar, butter or margarine, eggs and lemon (juice and zest) in the well and use a hand-held electric whisk to beat everything together. Start in the very centre of the well with the whisk on the slowest setting, then gradually increase the speed and incorporate the ingredients a little at a time until you have a soft, smooth, perfect cake mixture. This shouldn't take more than a minute or so.
3 Scoop the mixture into the tin and smooth the surface with the back of a spoon. Bake for about 1 hour, or until a skewer or sharp knife inserted into the cake comes out clean, and turn the cake out onto a cooling rack while it's still warm.
4 Use the skewer or sharp knife to make small holes over the surface of the cake (and the accent is on small here, you don't want your

cake to be full of craters or potholes) so the drizzle can seep into the sponge.

5   To make the drizzle, put the lemon juice and zest into a bowl and gradually add the icing sugar to the juice until you've got an opaque glaze. Don't try and add the juice to the icing sugar or you could end up with too-thick glacé icing instead.

6   Spoon the drizzle all over the surface of the cake and leave it to dry out and cool completely for about half an hour, then store in an airtight tin for a few days.

Coconut and Mallow Fluff Cake

Make the marshmallow first to give the setting process a head start while you get on with the cake. It can be stored at room temperature for a couple of days, so you can even make it well in advance.

8oz (225g) margarine
8oz (225g) caster sugar
4 eggs
½ teaspoon salt
3fl oz (75ml) milk
1 teaspoon vanilla extract
8oz (225g) self-raising flour
1 sachet of gelatine
4oz (110g) icing sugar
1oz (25g) cornflour
redcurrant jelly (or any red jam)
desiccated coconut

1   Lightly grease and base-line two 7–8 inch (18–20cm) sandwich tins. Preheat the oven to 180C/350F/gas 4.

2   Put the margarine and sugar in a large mixing bowl and beat thoroughly for a few minutes with a hand-held electric whisk until pale and fluffy.

3   with the salt. In another small bowl or measuring jug, beat the egg
    yolks, 2 remaining eggs, milk and vanilla extract together, then add
    gradually to the creamed margarine and sugar, whisking on high
    speed all the time to stop the mixture from curdling.

4   Sift the flour into the bowl and fold in carefully with a large metal
    spoon. The mixture should have a soft dropping consistency, but
    if you think it's too stiff, stir in a little more milk until it feels right.

5   Divide the cake mixture evenly between the two tins and bake for
    20 to 25 minutes until the sponges are risen and golden.

6   While the cakes are cooling, pour 2fl oz (55ml) very hot water into
    a small bowl or cup and sprinkle in the gelatine, whisking with
    a fork for a few seconds while the gelatine crystals dissolve.

7   Sift the icing sugar and cornflour together and use about a
    dessertspoonful to dust the inside of a large plastic lunchbox
    or bowl.

8   Whisk the egg whites until stiff enough to stand up in peaks.
    Add half the sifted sugar and cornflour to the bowl, whisking
    thoroughly again, then repeat the process with the remainder
    of the sugar/cornflour.

9   Add the liquid gelatine to the bowl in a steady trickle, folding it
    in with a metal spoon until it's completely incorporated and looks
    exactly like white emulsion paint. Pour into the plastic lunchbox,
    cover loosely with a tea towel and leave to set for about 2 hours
    at room temperature.

10 Once the marshmallow is completely set, break it up and fluff
    with a fork. Spread one of the sponge cakes with redcurrant
    jelly or jam and the other one with about half the quantity of
    marshmallow. Sandwich the cakes together and top with the rest
    of the marshmallow fluff, flattening it down with a blunt knife
    and smoothing it round the edges as best as you can. Don't worry
    if it looks a bit more like cottage cheese than marshmallow.

11 Cover with a thick layer of desiccated coconut and that's it.
    Cake magically transformed.

S'mores

Pink and white Princess marshmallows are another of my favourite
sweet things (see also chocolate and meringue), and perfect for
making into s'mores. In case you haven't discovered s'mores yet,
they're an American invention, wouldn't you know, and so-called
because they say you'll want 'some more' after eating the first one.
Anyway, after many happy hours of experimentation, I've found
that plain, home-baked biscuits made with a 2-inch (5cm) pastry
cutter work best – the lemon and almond thins (page 56) and
digestives (page 51) are ideal – or you can cheat and use Maryland
cookies, which are also the perfect size and shape for the job. Most
shop-bought biscuits tend to be too big, and although you can make
s'mores with bite-size biscuits, you have to use mini marshmallows,
which don't melt and stay gooey anywhere near as well as regular
marshmallows. Just perfect for a little girl's sleepover party, or a big
girl's night in.

To make 12
24 plain (preferably homemade) biscuits
2oz (50g) Green & Black's 70% dark chocolate
1 packet (200g) Princess pink and white marshmallows (or similar)

1. Put half a dozen biscuits upside down on a dinner plate. Grate
   the chocolate and put a teaspoonful (or as much as you can
   squeeze on) in the middle of each one, to allow room for melting.
   Top with a marshmallow.
2. Microwave on medium setting for 5 – 10 seconds until the
   marshmallow puffs up into a ball, twice the usual size.
   (Keep watching.) Lightly press another biscuit on top of each
   marshmallow – the right way up this time – and serve.

Virtually Fat-free Coffee and Walnut Cake

Fat-free cakes are no trickier to make than any other kind of sponge, but they're a bit less robust so you need to take more care getting them out of the tin and handling them afterwards. It also works better if you make this cake in a very large mixing bowl, which gives you a much wider surface area to sift the flour into at Step 4. For the cake to be as light and airy as it should be, it's important to sift the flour in gradually and not lose too much of the volume created by 5 minutes of whisking the sugar and eggs together. If you've ever accidentally dropped the flour into the bowl all at once, as I have, you'll know the mixture collapses completely and the cake doesn't rise properly in the oven.

> 4 teaspoons instant coffee
> 6oz (175g) self-raising flour
> 4 eggs
> 6oz (175g) caster sugar
> 2–3 tablespoons Quark
> 4 tablespoons icing sugar
> 8 walnut halves

1 Lightly grease and line the base of two sandwich tins. Preheat the oven to 180c/350f/gas 4.
2 Dissolve the instant coffee granules in 2 tablespoons hot water. Sift the flour once, then tip all the flour back into the sieve and stand the sieve on a plate ready for sifting again at Step 4.
3 In a very large mixing bowl, beat the eggs and sugar with a hand-held electric whisk for about 5 minutes until pale, fluffy and voluminous. When you lift the whisk up over the bowl and trickle the mixture across the surface, it should make a trail.
4 Sift the flour in very gradually, using a large metal spoon to fold the flour into the mixture. When the flour has all been incorporated,

slowly pour in about half the amount of dissolved coffee and carefully stir that in too.

5   Pour the mixture into the two sandwich tins, gently smoothing the surface with the back of a spoon. Bake for about 20 minutes until the sponges are risen and just golden.

6   Let the cakes cool in the tins for a while, then run a blunt knife around the edges and carefully turn them out onto a wire cooling rack. If you turn the cakes out onto a wire rack when they're still hot, they'll stick and you'll tear the surface when you try and lift them.

7   Once the cakes are completely cold, sandwich them together with the Quark. Make a glacé icing by sifting the icing sugar into a bowl, then adding the rest of the coffee and a few drops of cold water to get the icing to the right consistency. Ideally, it should be thick enough to cover the top of the cake completely, but runny enough to trickle down the sides.

8   Spread the icing over the top of the cake, smoothing it over with a blunt knife, and top with the walnuts. Store in the fridge.

Wheat-free Orange Cake

This is one of my favourite plain sponge recipes. It's also nice to know you can have your cake and eat it without wheat or dairy.

zest and juice of 2 oranges	6oz (175g) dark brown sugar
8oz (225g) rice flour	3 large eggs
1 teaspoon baking powder	1oz (25g) ground almonds
6oz (175g) butter	2 tablespoons flaked almonds

1   Lightly grease and long-strip-line a small 8 inch (20cm) square cake tin (see page 13). Preheat the oven to 190C/375F/gas 5.

2   Finely grate the rind and squeeze the juice of both oranges into a small cup or bowl. Sift the flour and baking powder together.

3   Cream the butter and sugar together with a hand-held electric whisk until pale and fluffy, then gradually add the beaten eggs, whisking continuously so the mixture doesn't curdle.

4   Use a large metal spoon to fold the ground almonds, flour and baking powder into the mixture, then add as much of the orange juice as you need to get a soft dropping consistency. (You may not need it all.)

5   Scatter the flaked almonds across the top and bake for about 30 minutes until the top is firm and golden. A skewer or sharp knife inserted into the middle of the cake should come out clean.

6   Allow the cake to cool for a few minutes, then lift it onto a wire rack to cool completely. Keeps in an airtight tin for a few days.

Eggless Fruit Cake

Some eggless cakes lack substance, but the addition of the sultanas and spices makes this every bit as good as a regular fruitcake with the advantage of having a lighter texture. So it's all good news, especially if you're trying to reduce your cholesterol – or you've run out of eggs. This is quite a shallow cake in an 8–9 inch (20–23cm) cake tin, so a smaller tin, say 6–7 inches (15–18cm), would be perfect.

8oz (225g) self-raising flour
1 teaspoon baking powder
¼ teaspoon bicarbonate of soda
1 big teaspoon mixed spice
1 big teaspoon cinnamon
4oz (110g) margarine
4oz (110g) sultanas (or mixed fruit)
4oz (110g) soft brown sugar
1 tablespoon lemon juice
¼ pint (150ml) or 1 small carton of natural yoghurt

1   Line the base and sides of a lightly greased round cake tin with greaseproof paper or baking parchment. Preheat the oven to 170C/325F/gas 3.

2   Sift the dry ingredients (flour, baking powder, bicarbonate of soda, mixed spice and cinnamon) into a large mixing bowl. Rub in the margarine in small pieces with your fingers until the mixture resembles medium-fine breadcrumbs.

3   Mix in the fruit and sugar and make a well in the centre.

4   Stir the lemon juice into the yoghurt, then add the soured yoghurt to the bowl. Use a wooden spoon or plastic spatula to gently beat the mixture together to a soft dropping consistency (add a table-spoon or two of milk if you think your mixture is a little too stiff).

5   Scoop the mixture into the prepared cake tin and smooth the surface over to flatten the top.

6   Bake for 1 to 1½ hours, checking after an hour. When a skewer or sharp knife inserted into the middle of the cake comes out clean, it's done.

7   Allow the cake to cool inside the tin for 5 minutes, then turn it out onto a wire rack to cool completely. Keeps for about a week in an airtight tin.

Slummy

'1. A condition poorer than the acceptable norm. 2. Busy mum: short of time, patience, money, culinary expertise and saucepans.'

Some days, cooking seems like the easiest thing in the world. Other times, it feels like a chore, which wouldn't be a problem if you and yours didn't feel like eating. But that's not how it works. So we can count ourselves lucky that there are such things as gravy granules, stock cubes, oven chips, fish fingers, frozen vegetables, curry paste, packet soups, instant sauces, bread mixes, chopped tomatoes, tinned onions and lots of other things that do some of the work for you.

Cheat ingredients are the slummy mummy's best friend and we can also thank our lucky stars for microwaves, hand blenders, freezers, online deliveries and shops that stay open all hours. But the ultimate shortcut is getting somebody else to do the cooking for you. Otherwise, what, exactly, are friends and families for?

A year or two ago I read about college-run courses for new students who have absolutely no life skills, to the extent that they need to be taught how to boil an egg (why? have they never read Delia?) and make a bed. So I would ask just one question of every mother or mother-to-be who picks up this book: do you really want this to be your child in two, ten or twenty years' time?

In the interests of proving that not all young people are lazy and unmotivated, some of the recipes in this chapter were cooked by unsupervised teenagers and eaten and approved by adults. Although there are two points I ought to make. The first one is, I was hoping to find enough volunteers to cook every recipe for me and I failed. Secondly, I was disappointed, if not surprised, to discover that getting the girls to help out was much easier than persuading the boys.

That said, all these recipes are well within the capabilities of children over the age of 12. Also husbands, boyfriends, absolute beginners and intelligent monkeys. So whether you're a busy mum with a family to feed or a single girl who wants to eat something more substantial than another Cup-a-Soup, give them a whirl. And whenever you can, delegate.

Cheat's Kedgeree

Pop a pouch (or two) of Uncle Ben's Express in the microwave instead of cooking the rice from scratch, and kedgeree just got even easier. I love it, and this must surely be one of the best recipes for those times you're in a tearing hurry, but can't face another sandwich or, heaven forbid, a fast-food hit.

Feeds 4
1–2 onions
1 packet of smoked mackerel fillets
oil
2 teaspoons curry powder
3–4 tablespoons frozen peas
black pepper
parsley
lemon juice

1   Peel and finely chop the onion. Remove the skin from the mackerel, check carefully for bones and flake the fish.
2   Warm some oil in a very large pan and fry the onion and curry powder until the onion starts to soften, then add the fish and peas and cook for another minute.
3   Meanwhile, cook the rice according to the packet instructions.
4   Stir the cooked rice into the pan with the other ingredients and season with black pepper and parsley – dried or fresh. Sprinkle with lemon juice and serve warm.

Cut another stage out of the recipe by using ready-prepared frozen onions at Step 1 Add sesame seeds to the oil at Step 2 for added nutrients and a nuttier flavour.

Vegetable Soup

Use any kind of stock you like. Supermarket fresh, homemade fresh
(or frozen) or a stock cube (or two) dissolved in boiling water. I don't
buy pre-packed assorted vegetables very often, but they're a great
time saver and because there's no waste involved, they're still very
affordable. This is the definitive student or single girl soup, so they're
perfect for this recipe.

Serves 4–6
1 onion
2 large packets of mixed prepared vegetables
olive oil
1½ pints (850ml) chicken or vegetable stock
1–2 tablespoon tomato purée
croutons
grated cheese

Any or all of the following
1 teaspoon Marmite
2 teaspoons dried marjoram
2 teaspoons basil
2 teaspoons dried coriander leaf
¼ teaspoon cayenne pepper OR a couple of teaspoons of mustard

1   Peel and slice the onion and cut the vegetables into smaller,
    roughly same-sized chunks.
2   Warm a couple of tablespoons of oil in a large pan and fry the
    onion until slightly golden. Put the rest of the vegetables in the pan
    with the stock and tomato purée and stir.
3   Add whatever seasonings you want to use from the list, cover the
    pan with a lid and simmer gently for 15 to 20 minutes until the
    vegetables are just cooked but still firm.
4   Allow the soup to cool slightly, then either blend the whole lot or,
    if you want chunky soup, blend half the quantity of soup and mix
    the purée with the unblended half.

5   To serve, heat the soup without letting it boil and top with the Baked Croutons on page 87 or use ready-made or improvise with broken up breadsticks, crackers, crisp bakes or baked croutons. Sprinkle with grated cheese.

Club Sandwich

Club sandwiches are most often found on the menu in hotels and country clubs, so they tend to have a more upmarket image than they deserve. In fact, they can be made almost entirely from leftovers, which makes them the perfect slummy solution when you want something that feels more like a meal than a snack, but you don't want the bother of cooking.

To make 4 sandwiches
8 rashers of streaky bacon
12 slices of bread
1 large avocado
mayonnaise
French mustard
4oz (110g) cooked chicken or turkey (approx)
2–3 tomatoes
1 small English lettuce
olives
cocktail sticks

1   Grill the bacon and leave to cool on kitchen paper to absorb the grease.
2   Lightly toast the bread so it's just golden, then allow the toast to cool and crisp up a bit.
3   Mash the avocado and mix with a couple of tablespoons of mayonnaise. (Alternatively, mix the mustard directly into the mayonnaise with a small spoonful of honey).

4 Slice the chicken and cut the bacon rashers in half. Thinly slice the tomatoes.

5 Make each double-decker sandwich by spreading the first piece of toasted bread with the avocado-mayonnaise. Add lettuce, chicken or turkey, a second layer of toast spread with mustard, followed by bacon, sliced tomato and the final piece of toast.

6 Pierce each sandwich with four cocktail sticks, then cut into quarters diagonally so each quarter is secured. Put an olive on the tip of each cocktail stick and serve.

Baked Croutons

Always make croutons with stale bread; fresh bread doesn't hold its shape well and absorbs too much oil. (Oil in a spray can is ideal for this recipe.) You'll get more than enough croutons for one big family meal from these quantities, so make this amount, then eat some and keep some. Homemade croutons keep well in an airtight tin for up to two weeks.

> 4–6 slices of stale bread, preferably white
> 2 tablespoons oil
> 2 teaspoons dried parsley
> salt & pepper

1 Preheat the oven to 200c/400f/gas 6 and cut the bread into small cubes, discarding the crusts.

2 Brush or spray a baking tray with a little oil and spread out the cubes on the sheet a little way apart. Bake for about 10 minutes, checking about halfway through the cooking time and shaking the tray so the croutons are evenly toasted.

3 Sprinkle (or spray) the croutons with oil and season with the parsley and salt and pepper while still warm.

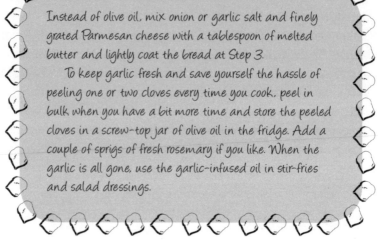

Instead of olive oil, mix onion or garlic salt and finely grated Parmesan cheese with a tablespoon of melted butter and lightly coat the bread at Step 3.

To keep garlic fresh and save yourself the hassle of peeling one or two cloves every time you cook, peel in bulk when you have a bit more time and store the peeled cloves in a screw-top jar of olive oil in the fridge. Add a couple of sprigs of fresh rosemary if you like. When the garlic is all gone, use the garlic-infused oil in stir-fries and salad dressings.

Oven-Baked Omelette

Pop this easy oven-baked omelette into the oven a few minutes after a tray of oven chips and they'll be ready at the same time. Needless to say, you can swap the ingredients around to suit yourself. Add a few mushrooms or replace the spinach with peas or asparagus.

Serves 4–6
oil
1 onion
butter
a couple of handfuls of spinach
salt & pepper
½ teaspoon nutmeg
4 slices of ham
cold leftover potatoes
6 large eggs
2oz (50g) cheese

1   Preheat the oven to 200c/400f/gas 6 and liberally grease a large Pyrex ovenproof dish with butter.

2   Warm a little oil in a large pan. Peel and slice the onion, then fry
    for a few minutes until golden.
3   Melt a tablespoonful of butter in the pan, then add the torn up
    spinach with a sprinkling of black pepper and nutmeg. Cook for
    a minute or two until the spinach has softened.
4   Dice the ham and cut the potatoes into fairly thick slices.
5   Mix the beaten eggs in a bowl with a splash of water, then pour
    the eggs into the prepared ovenproof dish. Add the onions, spinach,
    ham and potatoes. Stir with a fork to mix everything together and
    bake for 25 to 30 minutes until the top is golden brown and the
    omelette is set.

Packet Mix Pizza

Until now, whenever I made pizza dough with yeast, I left it to prove
for an hour before knocking it back – the way I would for bread –
and what a silly mistake that was.

My daughter Eleanor and her friend Amy made these pizzas with
a packet of bread mix, rolling the bases out straight away without
waiting for the dough to double in size, and the result was exactly
the same. Now I don't know whether to be pleased I've learnt a new
shortcut or livid because I didn't think of it myself a lot sooner (see
also Frozen Fish Pie on page 94).

Serves 4–6
1 packet of bread mix (1lb/450g)
1oz (25g) butter or margarine
10fl oz (275ml) warm water
flour (strong bread flour or plain), for kneading and rolling out
tomato purée
garlic purée

Suggested toppings

cheese and tomato	bolognese or chilli
sausage and tomato	meatballs, peppers and onion
chorizo and mushroom	spinach and ricotta
gammon and pineapple	mushroom and caramelised red onion
tuna and sweetcorn	mixed olives and green pesto
prawns and crab meat	mixed beans and red pesto

1   Make the dough according to the instructions on the packet i.e. empty the whole bag of bread mix into a large mixing bowl and rub in the butter or margarine with your fingertips until the mixture resembles medium-fine breadcrumbs. Add the water and mix to a fairly soft dough with your hands, then thoroughly knead the dough on a floured surface for about 10 minutes.

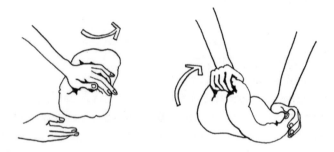

2   Lightly oil two large round tins (approximately 10 inches/25cm in diameter) or two large rectangular baking trays and preheat the oven to 190C/375F/gas 5.

3   Roll the dough out to roughly the same size as the tins and use your hands to make the bases fit as perfectly as possible.

4   If your toppings are ready, spread the pizza bases with a mixture of tomato and garlic purée – 3 tablespoons of tomato and ½ tablespoon of garlic purée per pizza would be about right – cover with the toppings and bake in the oven for 15 to 20 minutes. If you're cooking the pizzas later on, brush the surface of the dough with a little olive oil, cover with clingfilm and store in the fridge.

Cheese and Tomato Pie

This is a lot like quiche, but more British somehow, maybe because the breadcrumbs and flour add a bit of stodge, which some people talk about in such derisory terms you'd think a few extra carbs were as bad for your health as a Class A drug. Anyway, I've always been a girl who likes a bit of stodge, and for my money, a piece of pie is as good a way as any of making even the dreariest vegetables more attractive. This is lovely served hot with boiled potatoes and greens, or cold with salad.

Serves 4–6
1 onion
2 teaspoons plain flour
salt & pepper
3 eggs
3oz (75g) cheese
3oz (75g) breadcrumbs
3 tomatoes
1 ready-made pastry case
3½fl oz (100ml) milk or a mixture of milk and single cream

1   Preheat the oven to 200c/400f/Gas 6.
2   Finely chop the onion and mix it in a bowl with the seasoned flour. Add the eggs, cheese and breadcrumbs and whisk everything together with a fork.
3   Thinly slice the tomatoes.
4   Pour the mixture into the pastry case and cover with a layer of sliced tomatoes.
5   Bake for about half an hour until the top is golden in places and the filling is obviously set.

Reconstructed Lasagne

What do you do when there isn't enough lasagne to go round? Try topping whatever you've got with thinly sliced tomatoes and serve it up on a bed of spinach and mushrooms. That's it. Extra layers, added vitamins and more for everyone in a matter of minutes.

lasagne (freshly made or leftovers)
3–4 tomatoes
1oz (25g) butter
1 large bag of spinach (weight doesn't matter)
1lb (450g) mushrooms (or more)
1 teaspoon nutmeg
salt & black pepper

1 If you're warming up leftover lasagne, cover and reheat thoroughly in the oven or microwave.
2 When the lasagne is hot, remove the cover, top with the thinly sliced tomatoes and place under a preheated grill for a few minutes until the tomato cooks and colours.
3 Meanwhile, melt the butter in a large pan. Tear up the spinach and slice the mushrooms.
4 Fry the mushrooms for a couple of minutes, then add the spinach to the pan and season with nutmeg, black pepper and a pinch of salt. Cook for a couple more minutes until the spinach has wilted.
5 Serve with lots of salad or extra vegetables (broccoli or sweetcorn are ideal).

The Ultimate Fish Finger Sandwich

Make your own fish fingers whenever you can (see page 146), but as this is a slummy recipe there's no reason why you should feel bad about using shop-bought. Always buy fish fingers made from whole fillets if you can. The cheapest ones are a mishmash of fillers mixed with more unsavoury bits of the fish, and best avoided. My perfect fish finger sandwich is made with 'best of both' medium sliced bread, but use whichever kind you prefer. As a rough guide, I'd say use three to four fish fingers per sandwich.

To make 4 sandwiches
fish fingers
fresh spinach
8 slices of bread
horseradish sauce (from a jar)
lemon juice
2 tomatoes, sliced
1–2 oz (25–50g) Emmental cheese, sliced
Heinz salad cream
black pepper

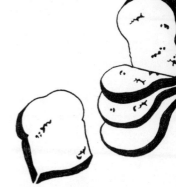

1 Grill the fish fingers for a few minutes on each side, according to the instructions on the packet.
2 Meanwhile, tear up the spinach into small pieces, but don't bother to cook it. It will wilt naturally next to the warm fish fingers.
3 Make each sandwich by spreading one slice of the bread with horseradish sauce. Add the fish fingers sprinkled with lemon juice, followed by the spinach, tomato and cheese, in that order. Top with salad cream, black pepper and the second piece of bread, cut and serve warm.

Frozen Fish Pie

Whenever I used frozen fish to make a pie, I always cooked it first.
Then a friend told me she once put the frozen fish straight into the
oven by accident and the pie turned out fine, so I tried it, and sure
enough, it works. Imagine my surprise then, when I had a proper
look at the packaging afterwards and discovered that frozen fish
pie is actually a perfectly safe and legitimate recipe in its own right,
and not the brainchild of resourceful cooks who have no need of
the manufacturers' instructions.

Anyway, the upside is that since fish pie just got even easier,
there's no reason why your children can't make it for you, and if
you have leftover mash in the fridge or you don't mind occasionally
using instant, they don't even have to cook the potatoes.

Feeds 4–6
1 small packet of instant mash or 4 large potatoes
butter
a handful of grated cheese
salt & pepper
6 frozen white fish fillets, skinned and boned
1 small packet of frozen prawns
frozen sweetcorn
spinach, fresh or frozen
1 tin of condensed asparagus soup
1 cup of milk (approx)

Any or all of the following
lemon juice
a small glass of white wine
chopped parsley

1   If you're cooking potatoes from scratch, peel them (or just leave
the skins on), cut into quarters and bring to the boil in a saucepan
of cold water. Simmer for a few minutes until the potatoes are
just cooked all the way through i.e. a sharp knife should go easily

through the middle (don't boil them too ferociously and turn the whole lot to mush). Otherwise, make up the instant mash according to the instructions on the packet. Whatever kind of potatoes you're using, add a spoonful of butter, a handful of grated cheese and salt and pepper according to taste.

2   Preheat the oven to 180c/350f/gas 4. Separate the frozen fish fillets and spread them out in a large ovenproof dish. Cover with the frozen prawns, a couple of handfuls of sweetcorn and roughly the same amount of spinach.

3   Pour the tin of condensed soup into a bowl, then fill the empty tin with milk, pour in and blend with a fork. Add lemon juice, white wine, parsley and any other seasonings you want to use.

4   Pour the liquid over the rest of the ingredients, then cover the entire surface of the pie with a layer of cooled mashed potato.

5   If you want to cook the pie later on, make sure the potato on top is completely cold, then cover with a layer of foil, shiny side inward, and keep it in the fridge.

6   Bake the pie for 30 minutes with the foil on, then remove the foil and cook the pie for a further 15 to 20 minutes until the potato is brown in places and the sauce is bubbling. Serve with peas or salad.

Matt's Mango Chicken

This recipe was devised by my son's friend, sixteen-year-old Matt Weatherley, who came up with the idea one night when he was looking around for something to make dinner with at his house. Since Matt and Billy first cooked this for me, I've made it a few times. It's completely delicious hot or cold and so straightforward it's easy to see how a couple of layabout boys can do it without even unplugging their iPods.

If you've got a fresh mango slightly past its best in the fruit bowl, try adding a few chunks of fruit – or just some of the juice – with the mango chutney at Step 3. Half a large, leftover cooked chicken works just as well as fresh fillets.

Serves 4–6
olive oil
4 chicken breast fillets
I orange pepper
I yellow pepper
½ jar of mango chutney
2–3 handfuls of cashew nuts

1 Warm a couple of tablespoons of oil in a very large saucepan or a wok while you dice the chicken.
2 Fry the chicken in the hot oil, turning frequently so the meat doesn't stick, while you cut up the peppers.
3 Add the peppers to the pan followed by the mango chutney and stir well. Cover the pan with a lid and simmer very gently for about 10 minutes until the chicken is cooked through.
4 Add the cashew nuts and cook for another 5 minutes. Serve with rice or noodles.

Piri Piri Chicken

This is a very family-friendly piri piri chicken recipe. For a hotter version, add a couple more chillies or just use stronger chillies and leave the seeds in.

Serves 4
4 chicken breast fillets
2 red peppers
2 red chillies
2 cloves of garlic
oil
1 large glass (approx 7fl oz/200ml) of wine
a handful of pitted black olives
fresh or dried parsley

1   Wash the chicken fillets, trim any little fatty bits off with a pair of kitchen scissors and cut the meat into strips. Cut the peppers and chillies into thin strips and crush the garlic.
2   Warm a couple of tablespoons of oil in a large pan and brown the chicken in two or three batches, keeping the cooked chicken warm in an ovenproof dish on top of the oven as you go.
3   When the chicken is done, add some more oil to the pan and fry the pepper, chilli and garlic for a few minutes. Add the wine and bring to the boil.
4   Turn the heat down and put all the meat in the pan with the olives, then cover the pan with a lid and simmer gently for 15 to 20 minutes until the meat is completely tender. Serve with salad and crusty French bread.
5   Garnish with plenty of parsley and serve with salad and crusty bread.

Turkey and Quinoa Rissoles

Unlike rissoles made with beef mince, these are better without breadcrumbs, and because they're baked in the oven rather than fried, they're even easier to make in a hurry.

This is one of those recipes that ticks all the boxes if you're trying to cut calories, but don't want to eat food that makes you feel as if you're actually on a diet. Quinoa on its own is pretty bland though, so if you don't like Tabasco sauce, spice the rissoles up with mustard, cayenne pepper, curry powder or anything that adds a bit of much-needed flavour.

Serves 4
1 mug of quinoa
1lb (450g) turkey mince
Tabasco sauce
dried or fresh parsley
salt & pepper

1 Rinse a mugful of quinoa in a sieve under cold running water and put it in a saucepan with 4 mugfuls of cold water (use the same mug each time to get the quantities right).
2 Bring to the boil, then cover with a lid and simmer for about 15 minutes until approx three-quarters of the water has been absorbed and the quinoa is translucent and separated into little white spirals. This isn't as baffling as it sounds and makes perfect sense once it's cooked. Preheat the oven to 200c/400F/gas 6.
3 As soon as the quinoa is cool enough to handle, put it in a bowl with the turkey mince, lots of Tabasco sauce, parsley, pepper and a little salt and squish it all together with your hands.
4 Shape the mixture into same-size balls with your hands and place on an oiled baking tray.
5 Bake for about half an hour until the rissoles are crisp and golden on the outside. Serve hot with mash and vegetables or a tomato-based pasta sauce or cold with spicy fried potatoes and salad.

Quinoa (pronounced 'keen-wah') is a protein-rich seed from the Goosefoot plant, which was discovered in South America by the Incas thousands of years ago. It's often thought of as a grain because it can be substituted for other grains – couscous and rice for example – in cooking. Low in carbohydrates and high in unsaturated fats, it's a powerful antioxidant and gives any recipe a nutrient boost.

Pork in Plum Sauce

I call this pork in plum sauce even when I make it with prunes because the idea of anything cooked in prunes is a bit off-putting. You can make it with fresh plums or even dried prunes stewed in a little water, but if you use tinned prunes, the syrup or juice does most of the work for you. This recipe is perfect for using up the dregs of the Cold Spiced Red Wine on page 234.

> 1–2oz (25–50g) butter
> 1–2 pork fillets per person
> 1–2 tins prunes or 1lb (450g) fresh plums

1   Melt the butter in a large pan and quickly brown the pork fillets. Transfer to a casserole dish, cover with a lid and cook in a very low oven (170c/325f/gas 3) for 1 to 1½ hours.
2   About halfway through the cooking time, push the prunes through a sieve, then pour the purée over the meat, replace the lid and continue to cook until the pork is completely tender. Serve with mashed potatoes and vegetables.

Gammon and Pineapple

For this recipe, it's easier to cut up the gammon before it goes into the oven so you can serve it straight up without the bother of carving once it's cooked. Cooking it in the syrup part of the way through means the meat stays nice and moist too.

If you want to serve the gammon and pineapple with oven chips, put the chips in about half an hour from the end (before you cover the meat with the syrup and pineapple at Step 3) and turn the oven up to 200C/400F/gas 6.

Serves 4–6
1½lb (700g) joint of gammon
1 small tin of pineapple chunks in natural juice
1 level tablespoon soft brown sugar
2 tablespoons soy sauce
splash of lemon juice

1   Preheat the oven to 190C/375F/gas 5. Remove the string from around the gammon, trim the fat off the meat and cut into roughly six thick slices (there'll be a few odd chunks as well).
2   Put the meat in a shallow ovenproof dish and cover with a layer of foil, shiny side inward. Cook for approximately half an hour.
3   Empty the tin of pineapple chunks into a bowl and add the sugar, soy sauce and lemon juice. Remove the foil and pour everything over the gammon. Bake for another 20 minutes. Serve with chips, sweetcorn and tomato wedges.

Shortcut Moussaka

Mushrooms aren't a classic moussaka ingredient, but I put them in whenever I find a few going brown at the bottom of the salad drawer (which is quite often for some reason). I've also made this with leftover roast lamb cut into small chunks instead of the mince. This is the slummy version of moussaka, so the topping is a quick one.

Serves 4–6
1 large aubergine
2 red onions
mushrooms
2 handfuls of spinach
olive oil
1lb (450g) lamb mince
1 tin of chopped tomatoes
2 tablespoons tomato purée
2 cloves of garlic
1 teaspoon cumin (seeds or ground)
½ teaspoon ground cinnamon
½ teaspoon nutmeg
salt
2oz (50g) feta cheese
2oz (50g) Cheddar cheese
3 large eggs
½ large carton of natural yoghurt

1 Thinly slice the aubergine, then cut the slices into halves and leave to soak in a bowl of very salty water for about 15 minutes. Rinse thoroughly, drain and dry in an old clean cloth.
2 Meanwhile, peel the onions and slice with the mushrooms. Tear up the spinach.
3 Preheat the oven to 190C/375F/gas 5.
4 Warm plenty of olive oil in a very large pan and quickly fry the aubergine pieces in two or three lots, transferring them to a large ovenproof dish when they're brown and quite crisp.
5 Put the onion and mushroom in the pan with some more oil and cook for a couple of minutes until the onion is at least soft, and preferably golden. Place in the ovenproof dish with the aubergine.
6 Brown the lamb mince in the pan and strain off as much excess liquid as you can once the meat is cooked through. Add the torn spinach leaves, chopped tomatoes, tomato purée, garlic, spices

and seasoning to the pan, stir well, then empty the pan into the ovenproof dish and thoroughly mix everything together.

7   Crumble the feta cheese and grate the Cheddar into a bowl with the beaten eggs and yoghurt, mixing well. Spoon the sauce over the moussaka, filling up any big gaps on the surface with more cheese. Bake for about 25 minutes until the cheese is brown and bubbling.

Lamb and Apricots

I got this idea from a friend who makes her version of the recipe with chicken fillets and tinned peaches.

Serves 4
sunflower oil
2lb (900g) lamb neck fillet
1 tin of apricots (11oz/300g) in natural juice
1 packet (4oz/110g approx) dried vegetable soup mix
1 pint (570ml) lamb stock OR ½ pint (275ml) each stock and apple juice

1   Warm a couple of tablespoons of oil in a very large pan. Preheat the oven to 150–170C/300–325F/gas 2–3.
2   Trim any fat off the lamb if there is any and cut the meat into medallions or large chunks. No need to season the meat, the soup mix is salty enough.
3   Brown the meat in the hot oil and put it in an ovenproof casserole dish with the entire contents of the tin of apricots emptied over it.
4   Make up the soup mix with the boiling hot stock (or the stock and juice) and pour over the meat and fruit.
5   Cover with a lid and cook the casserole in the oven for about 2 hours or until the meat is completely tender, stirring the sauce once about halfway through. Serve with rice or mashed potatoes and green vegetables.

Store Cupboard Shepherd's Pie

You can't beat a proper home-cooked shepherd's pie made with minced lamb, fresh rosemary and lots of mushrooms, but when you're down to your last few tins, green sprouting potatoes, a mouldy onion and an empty fridge, it's still possible to make a pretty good substitute for the real thing . . .

Serves 4
2 tins corned beef
1 tin baked beans
1 tin chopped tomatoes
fresh, frozen or tinned onions, garlic and tomato purée,
   if you have them
1 stock cube
1 packet of instant mashed potato

1   Preheat the oven to 190C/375F/gas 5.
2   Mash up the corned beef with a fork in a large ovenproof dish.
3   Add the baked beans, chopped tomatoes and onions, garlic or tomato purée, if you have them. Crumble in the stock cube and any seasoning you want to use. Soften the mixture with a little boiling water and give it a good stir to get everything well mixed.
4   Top the pie with the instant mashed potato made up according to the instructions on the packet.
5   Bake the pie for about 45 minutes until the sauce is bubbling and the potato topping is crisp and golden in places.

cook's tip

Make the mash slightly less slummy with the addition of a little milk or single cream, grated cheese or a couple of spoonfuls of cream cheese mixed with herbs.

Crunchy Minced Beef and Onion Pie

The crunchy part of this pie is a savoury alternative to the traditional sweet cheesecake base you'd make with digestive biscuits. It's one of those things I think of as my own idea, which usually means lots of other people are also thinking the same thing. Rough oatcakes can be quite thick or very thin, so it's hard to say precisely how many you'll need, but 6oz (150g) would be about right. Don't expect this pie to cut into slices like a cheesecake though, you have to spoon it out of the pan like a shepherds' pie.

Serves 4
1lb (450g) beef mince
1 onion
2 tablespoons tomato purée
rosemary (or any other seasoning)
6oz (175g) rough oatcakes
1oz (25g) butter or margarine
1oz (25g) grated cheese

1 Dry fry the mince with the finely chopped onion. As soon as the meat is cooked through and the onion has softened a bit, strain away as much of the oily liquid as you can. Stir in the tomato purée with the rosemary and whatever other seasonings you want to use.
2 Meanwhile, crush up the oatcakes with your hands and mix with the melted butter. Press roughly three-quarters of the mixture into the tin. (you need the rest for the topping).
3 Preheat the oven to 180c/350F/gas 4.
4 Cover the biscuit base with the meat, then mix the grated cheese with the remainder of the biscuit crumbs and sprinkle the whole lot over the top of the pie in a loose layer, like a crumble.
5 Bake for 20 to 25 minutes until the topping is crisp and golden and serve with baked beans or green vegetables.

Hot Beef Goulash

Use fresh onions and peppers if you like, but tinned Eazy fried onions and a jar of little red peppers (next to the olives in the supermarket) are perfect and cut the preparation time right down.

A heatproof casserole dish that you can use on the hob as well as in the oven is ideal here, otherwise start off with the largest pot or saucepan you've got, then transfer the goulash to a large ovenproof dish and leave it to slow-cook in the oven for a couple of hours.

And if further proof were needed that this is the easiest goulash recipe ever, my 12-year-old niece, Rachel, made it for six people and everyone said they loved it.

Serves 4–6
2 tablespoons flour
1–2 tablespoons paprika
oil
1½–2lb (675–900g) stewing steak
2 tins chopped tomatoes
1 tin Eazy fried onions
1 small jar of little red peppers
1 glass of red wine or sherry
2 tablespoons tomato purée
1 tablespoon garlic purée
2–3 bay leaves
salt & pepper

1 Preheat the oven to 170C/325F/gas 3.
2 Thoroughly mix the flour and paprika on a plate. Trim any little bits of excess fat off the meat (don't wash the meat first), then cut into roughly same-sized pieces.
3 Warm about 2 tablespoons of oil in the casserole or a very large pan while you coat the meat in the flour/paprika on the plate.
4 As soon as the oil is very hot, quick-fry the meat for a few minutes, turning it over frequently until it's browned on all sides.
5 Add the tinned tomatoes, onions, peppers, wine or sherry, tomato

and garlic purée, bay leaves and seasoning and bring to the boil.

6   Cover the goulash with a lid, then put it in the oven and cook for at least 2½ hours until the meat is completely tender. Serve with rice or garlic bread (or both).

Leftover Biryani

This is a great way of using up leftover meat from a joint of lamb or beef. Even if the meat was a bit tougher than you would have liked the first time round, this recipe gives you a second chance to make it perfect.

The biryani at my favourite local Indian restaurant comes with its own little omelette, which would be way too complicated for a slummy dinner, so I make one big omelette, cut it into quarters, and serve it underneath the curry with the salad garnish on top.

Serves 4
1lb (450g) leftover beef or lamb
2 potatoes
2 carrots
1 onion
2 cloves of garlic
oil
2 teaspoons curry powder
2 teaspoons ground cumin
2 teaspoons dried coriander leaf
1 teaspoon ground turmeric
1 pint (570ml) lamb or beef stock
1 tablespoon tomato purée
½lb (225g) mushrooms
1 small tin of peas (or frozen)
4oz (110g) basmati rice per person
4 large eggs
1 tablespoon butter
tomatoes and cucumber, to garnish

1   Dice the meat. Peel and cut the potatoes and carrots into medium-sized pieces. Slice the onion and crush or roughly chop the garlic.
2   Warm a couple of tablespoons of oil in a very large pan and fry the prepared vegetables and garlic for a few minutes until the onion has browned. Add the meat, spices, stock and tomato purée to the pan, bring to the boil then turn the heat right down and simmer the curry very gently for 1 to 1½ hours until the meat is completely tender.
3   Add the mushrooms to the pan about 20 minutes before the end of the cooking time.
4   Cook the rice separately, according to the packet instructions, and strain through a colander, rinsing well with boiling water to remove as much of the starch as you can.
5   Strain any excess liquid from the curry and add the cooked rice to the pan. Add the drained peas, stir well and keep the curry warm over a very low heat while you make the omelette.
6   Beat the eggs with a splash of water while you warm a tablespoon of butter in a large frying pan until it's brown and foaming. Pour the beaten eggs into the pan and cook over a medium heat until set, turning the omelette once if you can (otherwise finish it off under the grill).
7   Put a piece of omelette onto each plate, pile the mixed curry and rice over the top and garnish with tomatoes and cucumber, sliced or diced any way you like.

Magic Muffins

I didn't believe this recipe would work until it dawned on me that the main ingredients of ice cream are eggs, sugar and some kind of fat, so it figures that a very basic kind of cake can be made just by mixing ice cream and flour together.

These are muffins at their most simple and unsophisticated, but if there's a better recipe for very young children to make all by themselves, entirely unsupervised by you – unless you count watching from the sidelines with a cup of tea – I've yet to find it. Use a tablespoon to measure the ice cream if you don't have an ice cream scoop.

Makes 6–8 muffins
6 scoops of ice cream
6 tablespoons self-raising flour
sugar sprinkles

1   Take the tub of ice cream out of the freezer about 20 minutes beforehand or put the right amount of ice cream in a mixing bowl and leave for about 10 minutes to soften up.
2   Meanwhile, preheat the oven to 190C/375F/gas 5 and put paper muffin cases on a baking tray.
3   Beat the ice cream with a wooden spoon until it's really soft and runny, then sift in the flour and stir the mixture just enough to mix it.
4   Spoon the mixture into muffin cases, top with sugar sprinkles and bake for 10 to 12 minutes until the cakes are risen and golden.

Mini Doughnuts

Sometimes you just have to cook something without wondering if it's good for you, or even knowing why you want to cook it in the first place.

These doughnuts are a lot like the kind of sugary, greasy little dough balls that tempt you from a van in the market, and which you wouldn't dream of buying, but which suddenly acquire a veneer of respectability, albeit a thin one, if you make them yourself. These don't keep well and are best eaten straight away.

Makes around 16 doughnuts
2oz (50g) butter
2oz (50g) caster sugar, plus more for coating
2fl oz (55ml) milk
1 egg
½lb (225g) plain flour
2 teaspoons baking powder
oil

1   In a mixing bowl, cream the butter and sugar together with
a wooden spoon while you warm the milk in a small pan or in
the microwave for about 30 seconds. Pour the milk into the bowl
and stir until the butter has melted.
2   Whisk in the beaten egg, then sift in the flour and baking powder
and beat with the wooden spoon again to make a thick, dough-like
batter. Sprinkle some more sugar on a dinner plate.
3   Heat about 3 inches (7cm) of oil in a large, deep-sided pan and drop
dessertspoonfuls of the mixture into the hot oil, flipping them over
after a few seconds to brown them on both sides.
4   Drain the doughnuts on kitchen paper and roll them in the sugar
while still warm.

Snickerdoodles

As with flapjacks and jaffa cakes, it's hard to decide whether these
are cakes or biscuits. Really, I've got no right to call this lovely little
recipe slummy, but because snickerdoodles are much easier to make
than the end result would suggest, here they are.

Makes 24–30 biscuits

3oz (75g) margarine	1 teaspoon baking powder
4oz (100g) sugar	2 teaspoons soft brown sugar
2 eggs	2 teaspoons ground cinnamon
8 heaped tablespoons plain flour	2 teaspoons cream of tartar

1   Cream the margarine and sugar together in a mixing bowl with a hand-held electric whisk until pale and fluffy, then add the beaten eggs, a little at a time.
2   Sift the flour, cream of tartar and baking powder into the bowl and stir the mixture with a big metal spoon to make a soft dough. If the dough is too soft, sift in a little more flour. It should be soft, but firm enough to roll into a ball.
3   Wrap the dough in clingfilm or foil and keep it in the fridge for at least 2 hours until it's very chilled.
4   Preheat the oven to 200c/400f/gas 6 and lightly grease two large baking trays.
5   Mix the soft brown sugar and cinnamon together in a small bowl.
6   Break the dough up into walnut-sized pieces (or slightly larger) and form into balls with your hands. Roll the balls in the sugar and cinnamon mixture, then flatten them out slightly and place on the trays.
7   Bake for 10 minutes and allow to cool thoroughly before storing in an airtight tin. The snickerdoodles crisp up over a period of a couple of days and keep for well over a week.

Tray Bake Cake

The disposable aluminium oven trays you find in supermarkets and pound shops are ideal for making tray bake cakes, and as long as you wash them properly they should be good for at least two or three goes before you actually need to dispose of them. This amount of cake mixture is about right for a tray measuring 12 × 9½ × 2½ inches (30 × 24 × 6cm).

Makes about 24 squares
12oz (350g) self-raising flour
1 rounded teaspoon baking powder
6 eggs
6oz (175g) butter or margarine
6oz (175g) caster or soft brown sugar
6 heaped tablespoons icing sugar
1oz (25g) butter
a few drops of vanilla essence or food colouring
sweets, nuts or sugar sprinkles, to decorate

1   Preheat the oven to 180C/350F/gas 4. Lightly grease and long-strip-line the disposable oven tray with greaseproof paper.
2   Sift the flour and baking powder into a very large mixing bowl and make a well in the centre.
3   Put the beaten eggs, margarine and sugar into the well and use a hand-held electric whisk on high speed to beat everything together, starting in the very centre and gradually incorporating more and more of the dry ingredients until you have a smooth cake mixture. This only takes a minute.
4   Scrape the mixture into the prepared oven tray and bake for 45 minutes to 1 hour until the cake is set and springy and cooked all the way through. A skewer or sharp knife inserted into the middle of the cake should come out clean.
5   Allow the cake to cool completely in the oven tray.
6   Make the icing by sifting the icing sugar into a large mixing bowl and stirring in the melted butter with 2 tablespoons water. Gradually add another tablespoon of water until you have a smooth, workable icing, thin enough to spread easily over the surface of the cake and thick enough to give good coverage.
7   Before the icing has set completely, use a blunt knife to mark the cake into squares or rectangles, then decorate each segment with sweets and nuts or cover the whole lot with sugar sprinkles.

Earth Mummy

'1. Domestic Goddess type. 2. Ace baker, cook and homemaker (may induce boiling, simmering, steaming and stewing in other women).'

The earth mummy is a great cook and a regular little saint whose only slight flaws are permanently pink cheeks and a shiny nose from standing in front of the stove all day.

I'll never be her, although I'd like to be, and try to be sometimes – usually on a wet weekend when it's too cold and grey to be outside and cooking is a way to relax and unwind, rather than a routine task that needs to be done as quickly as possible.

The trick is to start thinking of your kitchen as a safe haven instead of a prison. Banish muddy football boots and similar unsightly objects to some other place so you won't be reminded of the less than appealing jobs you have to do. And don't worry about spending too many lonely hours on your own. If you can't enlist the help of a child or two to peel a few potatoes and keep you company, there's always the radio. You can also talk on your mobile, drink alcohol and operate a piece of kitchen machinery simultaneously without risking anyone's life or breaking the law.

And if a marathon cooking session doesn't sound like a whole lot of fun to you, look at it this way. In a single afternoon you can produce enough food to keep the family going

for at least three nights in a row. Or make twice that amount of child-size meals for the freezer, or enough baby food to last two months.

Twenty years ago, I left work a week before my first baby was due and spent the next few days cooking and freezing a six-week supply of dinners for two. I know I'll never reach those dizzy heights again. In any case, it was awful when we finally ran out of homemade ready meals and I had to start cooking every night again. But these days I still cook more than we need of pies, stews and sauces whenever I make them, then keep the excess in the fridge or freezer for another time.

Another earth mummy habit worth cultivating is slow cooking. Obviously, a proper slow-cooker is perfect for this if you have one (I don't), but all kinds of meat and vegetable casseroles, pies and pot roasts can be put together in minutes and left in the oven for a few hours. The preparation time is short and you get so much time off in the middle, it hardly feels as if you've cooked at all. Which is just another way of cheating when you think about it.

Finally, the phrase 'cooking from scratch' sounds very worthy and rather scary until you remember that to the Amish, anything that hasn't been baked, pickled, sown and grown in your own backyard is a cheat ingredient. So nobody truly produces meals from scratch any more unless they can reasonably claim they milked the cow, milled the flour, made the sausages and distilled the brandy all by themselves.

Pies

Fanatical healthy eaters would no doubt disapprove strongly of so much red meat and pastry, but I think they're more at risk of a heart attack worrying about the number of fat grams in a meat pie than the rest of us are eating one.

Although pies appear in various guises in the other chapters, I tend to want to make the heavier, heartier kind of pie when I've got a couple of hours to spare, a fridge full of meat and half a bottle of cider (sherry or wine) knocking around, so this is their natural home.

If the only reason you don't make many, or any, pies is because you worry about the pastry being too fiddly and time-consuming, forget it. The worst part, if you can call it that, is getting flour all over the worktop and making a rolling pin dirty. If I can be bothered to do that, I can usually be bothered to spend 5 minutes making the dough (that's all it takes). But when I can't be bothered, there's ready-made pastry. And when I can't even be bothered with that . . . well that's what slummy recipes are for.

Instead of pastry, sliced boiled potatoes and leftover mash both make a good topping for a pie, as does a savoury crumble mixture (see page 67), buttered stale bread cut into rounds or even a layer of sausagemeat, which can also be mixed with dried stuffing from a packet to stretch the meat a bit further and make a nice thick crust.

Mariners' Pie

This is a more deluxe fish pie than the frozen one on page 89. Not that it takes much longer to cook, there's just a bit more preparation involved, but it's worth it, and apart from lots of green vegetables swimming in garlic butter, the only other thing you need with it is a glass of dry white wine.

Serves 4–6

1lb (450g) potatoes
3 eggs
¾ pint (425ml) milk
2 bay leaves
salt & pepper
1lb (450g) any fresh white fish
dill
parsley
1 tablespoon butter
½lb (225g) mushrooms
1½ tablespoons plain flour
½ small carton of sour cream
2oz (50g) Cheddar cheese

1 Peel and cut the potatoes into halves (or quarters if very large), bring to the boil in a pan of cold water and simmer for a few minutes until just soft, in the usual way. Strain the potatoes and leave to cool on a clean surface.

2 Meanwhile, bring the eggs to the boil in a small saucepan and simmer for about 10 minutes to hard-boil.

3 In the same saucepan you used to cook the potatoes – no need to rinse it out – bring the milk to the boil with the bay leaves and a little salt and pepper, then add the fish fillets cut into large pieces and simmer for about 10 minutes until the fish is tender.

4 Remove the fish from the pan with a slotted spoon and put in a large ovenproof dish. Strain and reserve the milk. Flake the fish, removing any skin or bones.

5   Preheat the oven to 180c/350f/gas 4.
6   Peel and roughly chop the hard-boiled eggs, scatter over the fish
    and sprinkle with plenty of dill and parsley – fresh and finely
    chopped or dried – according to taste. Season with black pepper.
7   Melt the butter in a frying pan, add the finely sliced mushrooms
    and cook for a couple of minutes. Stir in the flour, cook for another
    minute, then pour on the reserved milk and bring to the boil,
    stirring continuously until the sauce thickens.
8   Take the pan off the heat and stir the sour cream into the sauce.
    Pour the sauce over the fish and arrange the thinly sliced boiled
    potatoes on top. Sprinkle with the grated Cheddar cheese and
    bake for about 15 minutes, until the top is golden.

Chicken Pie

You could also make this easy pie with shortcrust, rough puff
or ready-made puff pastry, but best of all is the Potato Pastry
(see page 154) if you have any leftover mash to use up. Needless
to say, this recipe is even more perfect if you also have leftover
cooked meat and homemade stock in the fridge.

Serves 4
¾–1lb (350–450g) potato pastry (approx) (see page 154)
1 bundle of asparagus
1lb (450g) mushrooms
1 tablespoon butter
1 level tablespoon plain flour
1lb (450g) cooked chicken
salt & pepper
2fl oz (55ml) meat or vegetable stock
milk, for glazing

1   Preheat the oven to 180c/350f/gas 4.
2   On a floured surface, roll out two-thirds of the pastry to line

a well-greased ovenproof dish, which should be large (about 9 inches/23cm square) and deep-sided. Prick the pastry with a fork and rest in the fridge with the remainder of the pastry wrapped in clingfilm while you make the pie filling.

3   Cut the asparagus spears into 2 inch (5cm) chunks and slice the mushrooms while you melt the butter in a large pan. Once the butter is golden brown and foaming, fry both vegetables until just soft, then stir in a tablespoon of flour and cook for another minute.

4   Put the chopped chicken in the pie followed by the vegetables. Season with salt and pepper and pour the stock all over the filling as evenly as you can to get a good distribution.

5   Roll out the remaining pastry to make a lid for the pie and use a little milk to press the edges down well. Glaze the whole surface of the pie with more milk and bake for 40 to 50 minutes until the pastry is crisp and golden.

Chicken and Sausagemeat Pie

If you think two kinds of meat is overdoing it, leave out the sausage-meat and fill the gap with sliced carrots and extra potatoes.

Serves 4
2¾–3lb (1.25–1.35kg) chicken thighs (on the bone)
3 tablespoons plain flour
salt & pepper
2lb (900g) potatoes
2 onions
6 large good-quality sausages
¾ pint (425ml) chicken stock (fresh, if possible)

1   Preheat the oven to 170C/325F/gas 3.

2   Remove the chicken skin and trim any little fatty bits off the meat. Dust the chicken thighs in seasoned flour while you warm some oil in a very large pan.

3   Peel and thickly slice the potatoes while you fry the finely chopped onions, browning the chicken thighs in batches at the same time.
4   Put a thin layer of potato slices on the bottom of a large casserole dish, cover with the chicken pieces and onions, followed by a second layer of potatoes.
5   Squeeze the sausages out of their skins and flatten the meat into rough patties with your hands, then put all the sausagemeat in the casserole.
6   Cover the layer of sausagemeat with a final layer of sliced potatoes and carefully pour the stock evenly over the whole lot.
7   Season with salt and pepper, cover the casserole with a lid and bake for up to 2 hours. Take off the lid, turn the oven up to 200C/400F/gas 6 and bake for another 15 to 20 minutes until the top layer of potato is well browned. Serve with green vegetables.

Fidget Pie

This is a very old recipe, traditionally made at harvest time. The name 'fidget' is said to have come from the fact that the pie was originally 'fitched' or five-sided. I serve it with baked beans, which is far from traditional, but never mind. That's the way I like it.

Serves 4
For the pastry
2oz (50g) Trex
1oz (25g) butter
6oz (175g) plain flour
2–3 tablespoons milk, plus more for glazing

2lb (900g) potatoes
1lb (450g) Bramley cooking apples (approx)
sunflower oil
1lb (450g) bacon
¼ pint (150ml) stock and cider (approx)

1 Make the shortcrust pastry by rubbing the fat into the flour with your fingers until the mixture resembles medium-fine breadcrumbs, then make a well in the centre and add a little milk to make a fairly soft dough. Rest the pastry at room temperature while you make the pie filling.

2 Peel the potatoes and apples, slicing the potatoes thinly and the apples thickly.

3 Meanwhile, warm a couple of tablespoons of sunflower oil in a pan, cut the bacon into small pieces and fry until brown and crisp. Preheat the oven to 180c/350f/gas 4.

4 In a large well-greased pie dish, put a layer of potatoes followed by the bacon, all the apples and a second layer of potatoes. Pour on enough of the stock to wet the filling, but not to cover everything – you may not need it all – then roll out the pastry on a floured surface to make the pie lid. Glaze the entire surface of the pastry with milk.

5 Bake the pie near the bottom of the oven for about 1 hour until the pastry is golden. Put a sharp, long-bladed knife through the pie. When the pie is cooked, the potatoes should be soft.

Spicy Pork Strudel

The cheats' way of making strudel is to use ready-made filo pastry, but strudel pastry is actually quite different from filo. Although it's very easy to make in the early stages, rolling this strudel pastry out thinly enough to get that lovely flaky texture does take a fair bit of patience and skill. But what does it matter if your pastry is less than perfect, especially if you've never made it before? Don't expect too much from it and you won't be disappointed.

Serves 4
For the pastry
8oz (225g) plain flour (plus more for rolling)

¼ teaspoon salt
2 tablespoons sunflower oil
melted butter

For the filling
1 cupful of cranberries
3 tablespoons sugar
4 sausages
1lb (450g) pork mince
1 big teaspoon ground ginger
1 big teaspoon ground cinnamon
1 level teaspoon chilli powder

1   Sift the flour and salt into a mixing bowl, make a well in the centre
    and add ¼ pint (150ml) lukewarm water with the oil, flipping more
    and more of the flour into the liquid and pinching the mixture
    together with your fingers to make a soft, sticky dough.
2   Knead the dough for a minute on a floured surface, then put it
    back in the bowl. Sprinkle in a bit more flour if the dough's too
    sticky to make a ball, but expect it to be slacker than other types of
    dough. Cover with a cloth and leave to stand at room temperature
    for an hour.
3   Meanwhile, put the cranberries in a small saucepan with the sugar
    and a very little water (just enough to stop the cranberries sticking
    to the bottom of the pan) and simmer gently for about 20 minutes
    until the fruit is soft and jammy. Allow the cooked fruit to cool
    completely before mixing with the meat.
4   Squeeze the sausages out of their skins and put the meat in a
    bowl with the pork mince, cooled fruit, ginger, cinnamon and
    chilli powder.
5   Preheat the oven to 190C/375F/gas 5 and lay a sheet of greaseproof
    paper on a large ovenproof tray.
6   Roll out the dough slowly and carefully on a floured surface to
    about 9 × 12 inches (23 × 30cm) until the dough is, ideally, thin
    enough for you to see your fingers through. Don't worry about the
    thick edges; you can trim those at the end. Repair any little rips or

tears as best you can and lift the pastry onto the greaseproof paper by rolling it over the rolling pin, then laying it down flat.

7 Brush the pastry all over with melted butter, then pack the filling into a long sausage down one side of the pastry, leaving a gap of about 1 inch (2.5cm) along the edge. Trim the other three edges of the pastry all the way round, then gently push the strudel into a roll, lifting the paper underneath to help you as you go. When you're almost at the end, tuck the edges in at either side, then continue rolling to the end.

8 Lift the strudel onto a large baking tray, still on the paper, liberally brush the pastry with the rest of the melted butter and bake for about 1 hour until the pastry is golden.

Lamb Stew and Herby Dumplings

Serves 4–6
2lb (900g) lamb neck fillet
black pepper
lard or oil
2 onions
4 large potatoes
1 small swede
a couple of carrots
2 tablespoons plain flour
1–1½ pints (570–850ml) lamb stock
1 teaspoon gravy powder

For the dumplings
4 tablespoons self-raising flour
¼ teaspoon salt
2 tablespoons suet
½ teaspoon dried mixed herbs
1 small handful of fresh mint

1   Trim the meat and season with a little black pepper while you warm some lard or oil in a very large pan and preheat the oven to 170C/325F/gas 3.
2   Slice the onions and chop the vegetables into roughly same-sized pieces (not too small though or they'll turn to mush in the oven).
3   Seal the meat in the hot oil as quickly as you can and transfer to a large casserole dish.
4   Fry the onion, potato, swede and carrot together, stir in the plain flour and cook for another couple of minutes before adding the vegetables to the casserole with the meat.
5   Make the stock and pour over the meat and vegetables.
6   Cover with a lid and cook in the oven for about 3 hours, or until the meat is completely tender. If the gravy is too watery at the end of the cooking time, mix the gravy powder to a paste with 2 tablespoons cold water and add to the stew to thicken.
7   Make the dumplings by mixing the flour, salt, suet, mixed herbs and chopped mint (use 2 teaspoons dried mint if you don't have fresh) together, gradually adding ½ mug cold water to make a soft, but not too sticky dough.
8   Roll the dough into dumplings with your hands and place them on top of the stew.
9   Cook the stew for another 20 minutes or so without the lid, until the dumplings are risen and slightly golden.

Lancashire Hot Pot

If you use lamb cutlets you can cut the cooking time down to about 2 hours, but I much prefer to use neck fillet, which is as succulent and juicy as more expensive cuts of meat as long as it's cooked long and slow enough. In fact, I don't think it's ever worth rushing the cooking when the preparation time is so short. That last half an hour or so makes the difference between the meat being just done and perfectly tender.

There's no definitive Lancashire hot pot recipe, which has many variations including the addition of kidneys or oysters, which were dirt cheap in Britain a couple of hundred years ago. Mutton, and even beef, has sometimes been used instead of lamb, also extra vegetables; carrots, swedes and turnips, for instance.

Serves 4–6
2lb (900g) potatoes
oil
1 large onion
2lb (900g) neck fillet of lamb
salt & pepper
1 pint (570ml) lamb or beef stock
butter
thyme
rosemary

1   Preheat the oven to 170C/325F/gas 3. Peel the potatoes, rinse them well and slice into rings about ⅛ inch (2mm) thick.
2   Heat some oil in a large pan, fry the chopped onion for a few minutes, then add the lamb and brown the meat quickly on all sides.
3   Put half the potato rings on the bottom of a deep ovenproof dish, cover with the lamb and onion and season well.
4   Pour in the hot stock, then layer the rest of the potatoes on top of the meat and dot with small pieces of butter.
5   Cover the casserole with a lid, or a sheet of foil, and cook in the low oven for a minimum of 3 hours, then remove the lid and continue cooking for another 15 to 20 minutes until the potatoes on the top are golden brown and crisp around the edges.

Cornish Pasties

Potatoes, onions and turnips are classic Cornish pasty ingredients, but here I've replaced the turnips with carrots. Lamb neck fillet works just as well as beef, so use whichever one you like (I guess it only really matters if you're Cornish and don't want to mess with tradition). One thing that does matter is the size and shape of the vegetables, so cut them up small and slice them thinly. That way you can pack more filling into the pasties. Bigger chunks create gaps, meaning you end up with too much air and not enough substance in every mouthful, which is never a good thing.

Makes 6 (plus a much smaller extra one with the trimmings)
1lb (450g) plain flour
1 teaspoon salt
6oz (175g) lard or Trex
2oz (50g) suet
10–12oz (275–350g) beef (braising, stewing or chuck steak) or lamb
  neck fillet
2 potatoes
2 carrots
1 onion
salt & pepper
1 egg
a big splash of milk

1 Put the flour and salt in a large mixing bowl and rub in the lard or Trex in small pieces. Mix in the suet, make a well in the centre and pour in 4fl oz (120ml) cold water, pinching the mixture together with your hands and kneading gently to make a firm dough. Cover the bowl with clingfilm or a cloth and leave the dough to stand at room temperature while you prepare the filling.

2 Trim any excess fat off the meat if there is any and snip the meat into tiny pieces with kitchen scissors. Peel the vegetables and cut into small pieces, then slice (not dice) them thinly and season well with salt and pepper.

3   Preheat the oven to 200C/400F/gas 6 and mix the beaten egg with a big splash of milk in a cup or small bowl.

4   Roll the pastry out on a lightly floured surface – not too thinly – and use a side plate roughly 7 inches (18cm) across to cut the pastry into six rounds, re-rolling the trimmings as necessary.

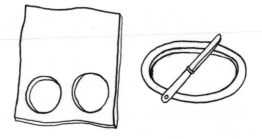

5   Wet the outside edges of each round with the egg mixture and put a tablespoonful of the mixed vegetables in the centre topped with a layer of meat. Close the pastry across the top and pinch the edges firmly together between finger and thumb to make a fluted crust.

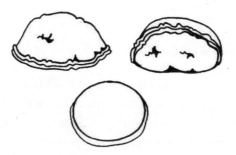

6   Put the pasties on a well-greased baking tray and brush well with the rest of the beaten egg. Bake for 10 minutes, then turn the temperature right down to 170C/325F/gas 3 for about 1 hour until the meat is tender. Delicious hot or cold.

Beef Pan Pie

This easy pan pie can feed twice the number of people with the same amount of effort if you use an even bigger pan and double up the quantities of all the ingredients except the pastry (although you may have to roll it out a little bit thinner if the circumference of the pan is also bigger).

Like every other recipe where you slow cook the meat for a few hours then go off and do something else, this doesn't even feel much like cooking, which makes it even more perfect.

Serves 4
3–4 tablespoons oil
1½lb (700g) stewing steak
1 large onion
1 leek
2 carrots
½ tablespoon butter
1 tin chopped tomatoes
¼ teaspoon salt
¼ teaspoon cayenne pepper
¼ pint (150ml) stock

For the pastry
4oz (110g) self-raising flour
2oz (50g) suet

1   Warm the oil in a very large pan over a high heat while you cut the meat into chunks and trim any excess fat, if there is anything. Brown the meat in the hot oil and set aside.
2   Meanwhile, peel and slice the onion, leek and carrots. When all the meat is done, melt the butter in the pan and fry the vegetables for a few minutes, then return all the meat to the pan with the chopped tomatoes, salt, cayenne pepper and stock.
3   Stir well, then turn the heat right down, cover with a lid and simmer very gently for about 1 to 1½ hours.

4   Mix the flour and suet in a bowl, then gradually add 2fl oz (55ml) water and pinch the mixture together to make a fairly stiff dough. Roll out the dough to make a circle roughly the same size as the surface of the pan, cutting around the lid to get it just right.
5   Lay the pastry circle on top of the stew, replace the lid and cook for another hour. Serve with mashed potatoes and peas.

Spinach and Meat Loaf

This isn't strictly a pie, but because it's very meaty and wholesome, and I usually make it in a round dish then cut it into slices, it feels like one to me. In fact, it's ideal for using up the remains of a ham or bacon joint and if you have a mixture of fresh herbs – sage, parsley, lemon thyme and rosemary all work well – so much the better. You can also use leftover roast pork instead of fresh mince if you have it.

Serves 4–6
1 bag of baby leaf spinach (225g/8oz approx)
½lb (225g) ham
1lb (450g) pork mince
1 small onion
2 cloves of garlic
1 tablespoon mixed herbs or herbes de Provence
1 level teaspoon nutmeg
black pepper
1 egg

1   Preheat the oven to 190C/375F/gas 5. Cook the spinach in as little water as possible for a couple of minutes, preferably in the microwave, then gently press dry to remove excess liquid and shred finely.
2   Chop the ham into very small pieces and put in a bowl with the minced pork, grated onion, crushed garlic, herbs, nutmeg, black pepper and beaten egg.

3   Squish the mixture together with your hands very thoroughly, then press the mixture into a round Pyrex casserole dish or grease a loaf tin with butter and use that instead.

4   Stand the dish in a shallow tray of boiling water (the water level should come at least halfway up the dish) and bake for about 1 hour. If you like, turn the cooked loaf out on to a baking tray, turn the oven up high and cook for another 10 minutes or so to brown the outside. Serve with mashed potatoes and vegetables.

Steak and Ale Pie

I could stand in the supermarket all morning reading the labels on bottles of ale – they're infinitely more interesting and imaginative than anything you'll ever find on a bottle of wine – and even though I'm no expert, I'd say you won't go far wrong with anything that includes the word 'Kentish'.

The easy rough puff pastry in Make Your Own (see page 153) is perfect for this recipe, or you can use ready-made puff pastry if you prefer. Cooking the pastry separately and putting it over the meat on the plate is one of my favourite cheats because it's quicker and less fiddly than making a proper lid for the pie.

Serves 4–6
2lb (900g) stewing steak or beef rump (or more)
4 tablespoons plain flour
salt & pepper
2 onions
oil
1 bottle of strong, dark ale (1 pint/570ml)
a big splash of soy sauce
2 beef Oxo cubes
pinch of cayenne pepper
1lb (450g) rough puff pastry (approx)

1   Cut the meat into roughly same-sized chunks and trim any excess fat. Sift the flour onto a dinner plate, season with salt and pepper and coat the meat in the seasoned flour. Peel and finely chop the onions.

2   Preheat the oven to 150C/300F/gas 2 and warm about 4 tablespoons oil in a very large pan.

3   Fry the meat in the hot oil in batches to seal in the juices, transfer to a large ovenproof casserole dish, then cook the onion in the same pan, adding a little more oil or a dessertspoonful of butter, if necessary.

4   When the onion is brown, put all the meat back in the pan and, keeping the heat up high, pour on the ale with the soy sauce and crumble in the Oxo cubes.

5   Stir well, add a pinch of cayenne pepper, cover the casserole with a lid or a layer of foil and cook near the bottom of the oven for about 3 hours or until the meat is completely tender.

6   On a floured surface, roll out the pastry to a thickness of about ¼ inch, trim the rough edges and cut the pastry into large squares – say one per person – or use a pastry cutter to cut out smaller rounds.

7   Meanwhile, turn the oven up to 190C/375F/gas 5. Place the pastry shapes on a greased oven tray and bake at the top of the oven for about 15 minutes until the pastry is well risen and golden. Once the pastry is cooked, spoon the steak and ale pie 'filling' onto the plates and top with a piece of pastry.

One final point I'd like to make on the subject of pies – it is one of my favourites after all – is that less than fifty years ago, when the population was slimmer and fitter with far fewer health problems than we have today, not only did most people eat them regularly, a pie for dinner was almost always followed by pudding and custard.

Make Your Own

Even if you're too busy to cook from scratch every day, most of the recipes in this section are so incredibly quick and easy – Yorkshire pudding, fish fingers and most of the bread recipes, for a start – you're bound to want to make them sometimes.

When you're really not in the mood for cooking, making your own toast feels too much like hard work, but if you've got the time to drag yourself to the supermarket for ready-made pastry, you've got time to make your own, with enough left over for a cup of tea and a quick lie down. I'm not going to pretend I get the urge to make my own yoghurt or fresh pasta very often, but it's good to know how to make the foods we eat often and generally take for granted, even if some of the suggestions for making your own in this chapter owe more to wishful thinking than the reality of daily life.

Bread

Making bread is very satisfying and a fun thing to do sometimes. It's also a great activity for children, which is why I wish I'd tried harder to make bread with mine years ago when they were little and I still had the chance. Instead, I used to start every summer holiday with a new bag of strong bread flour, a packet of dried yeast and the very good intention of making bread with my kids, my nieces and whoever else's children were around at the time, only to stick the ingredients at the back of the cupboard, fill up the paddling pool and forget all about it. Now it's too late for me to reinvent myself as a perfect *Little House on the Prairie* kind of mother, but it may not be too late for you.

Add a couple of tablespoons of dried herbs or seeds to any kind of bread. Mix approximately two-thirds into the dry ingredients or press into the dough at the kneading stage if you prefer, then use the remainder to scatter across the top just before the loaf goes into the oven.

- Seeds: pumpkin, sunflower, caraway, poppy, sesame or mixed.
- Herbs: rosemary, thyme or sage.
- Porridge oats: the same amount of porridge oats can be used separately, or in addition, to the herbs or seeds.

Quick Yeast-free Bread Rolls

A really basic recipe, but these little dinner rolls are great for
stretching leftovers a bit further and simple enough for children
to make on their own. Serve them up with a slummy main course
or some instant soup so it looks as if you've actually gone to a bit
of trouble instead of taking the easy way out (again).

Makes 6 rolls
½lb (225g) self-raising flour
½ teaspoon salt
½oz (10g) vegetable shortening, such as Trex or Cookeen

1   Preheat the oven to 220C/425F/gas 7 and lightly grease one
    oven tray.
2   Put the flour and salt in a large bowl, add the fat in small pieces
    and rub in with your fingertips until the mixture resembles
    medium-fine breadcrumbs.
3   Pour just under ¼ pint (150ml) water into the bowl and start
    mixing it together, adding the rest of the water or a little more
    flour and kneading well to make a stretchy dough.
4   Tear the dough into six roughly same-sized pieces and roll into
    balls. Place the rolls on the oven tray and bake for 15 minutes until
    crisp and golden on the outside. Allow to cool completely before
    breaking the rolls into rough halves and buttering them.

Irish Soda Bread

This is another easy recipe. There's no yeast involved and it doesn't
take much kneading – in fact the less handling the better – so it's
super-quick too. The cultured buttermilk you find in the supermarket
today is much like natural yoghurt, so use that instead if you'd rather.

1lb (450g) self-raising flour
1oz (25g) sugar
1 teaspoon salt
2 teaspoons bicarbonate of soda
1oz (25g) butter
¼ pint (150ml) milk
¼ pint (150ml) buttermilk or natural yoghurt

1 Preheat the oven to 180c/350F/gas 4 and lightly oil a baking tray.
2 Sift the flour, sugar, salt and bicarbonate of soda into a large mixing
   bowl, add the butter in small pieces and rub in until the mixture
   resembles medium-fine breadcrumbs. Make a well in the centre.
3 Pour all the milk and about half the buttermilk into the well,
   mixing with a blunt dinner knife or your hand and adding more
   buttermilk if necessary to make a soft dough. If you find it's a little
   sticky after you've added all the buttermilk, mix in a bit more flour.
4 Turn the dough onto a floured surface and knead very lightly for
   another minute before forming it into a round cottage-style loaf.
5 Place the loaf on the baking tray and use a sharp knife to mark
   a deep cross on top. Bake in the oven for 30 to 40 minutes and
   allow the loaf to cool for at least half an hour. Break into quarters,
   then either break the quarters into smaller pieces or cut into
   rough slices.

Potato Bread

Unlike Irish soda bread, this type of bread does need to be proved,
preferably overnight, but just think of the long proving part as down
time, rather than an inconvenience, because the method is as simple
and straightforward as any other kind of bread and the end result is
worth the wait.

Makes 2 loaves

4–6 medium-sized potatoes

1½lb (700g) strong bread flour (or more)

1 sachet of dried yeast

1 tablespoon salt

1 tablespoon natural yoghurt

1   Peel and boil the potatoes in the usual way, then drain before mashing them, setting the cooking water aside to cool slightly while you get the rest of the ingredients ready.

2   Sift the flour into a very large bowl with the yeast and salt.

3   Make a well in the centre of the flour, add the mashed potato, ½ pint (275ml) of the potato water and the yoghurt and mix it all together with your hand to form a soft, slightly sticky dough.

4   Turn the dough onto a floured surface and knead for a good 10 minutes, incorporating more flour as and when you need to.

5   Prove the dough in the fridge overnight. The best way is to put a few drops of oil inside a large food bag and rub the sides of the bag together to leave a thin film of oil on the sides, which makes it easier to get the dough out later on. Tie a very loose knot at the top of the bag so there's plenty of room left inside for the dough to expand.

6   Next day, when the dough has doubled in size, preheat the oven to 200c/400f/gas 6 and grease two loaf tins.

7   Turn the dough out onto a floured surface, knock it back and knead for a good 10 minutes again, same as the first time, then halve the dough, knead each half separately for a minute, form into roughly the right shape for your tins and gently press the dough into the tins.

8   Bake near the top of the oven for 5 to 10 minutes, then turn the oven down to 180c/350f/gas 4 for another 15 minutes. When you tip the loaves out of the tins and tap the underside, they should make a hollow sound, meaning they're done.

Ciabatta

Baking ciabatta is well worth doing in the summer months when you can create a little bit of Italy in your own back yard by proving the bread outside in the sun, which makes sense when you think about it. There can't be many Tuscan villages where everyone has an airing cupboard or an Aga. Anyway, it works for me, and it will work for you, as long as it's really hot and sunny and you keep the dough well covered and out of reach of passing cats and foxes.

Makes 2 loaves
1lb (450g) strong bread flour, plus more for kneading and dusting
1 sachet of dried yeast
2 teaspoons sugar
1 teaspoon salt
4 tablespoons olive oil

1 Sift the flour into a large mixing bowl with the yeast, sugar and salt; make a well in the centre and pour in ½ pint (275ml) warm, previously boiled water with the olive oil and mix to make a dough.
2 Turn the dough out onto a floured surface and knead well for at least 10 minutes, pulling a bit more flour in until the dough has lost any trace of stickiness and is completely smooth.
3 Divide the dough into two halves; shape each one into a rough oblong, place the loaves on a large oiled baking tray and cover with a very damp cloth. To stop the dough sticking to the cloth when it rises, stand a tall jar or something similar in the middle of the tray underneath the cloth to keep it up and away from the dough.
4 Leave the dough to prove for 1 hour, by which time it should be well risen and puffy and preferably doubled in size.
5 Preheat the oven to 200C/400F/gas 6. Sift a little more flour over the surface of the loaves and bake for 15 to 20 minutes until golden in colour.

Butter

I remember being taught how to make butter at school when I was very small, back in the days when all that was required of five- and six-year-olds was learning to read and write and do simple sums. The rest of the time was spent playing with water and sand and running around in the field outside.

Now poor primary school teachers are much too stressed by the demands of the ever-changing national curriculum to make butter, which probably wouldn't be allowed in any case as butter is surely at odds with Healthy Schools Status. (Perhaps today's Year One children get a lecture on the evils of saturated fats instead.)

There may not be much point in making your own butter – I can't claim it's a way of saving money or that the results are necessarily better than commercially produced butter – but it doesn't hurt sometimes to be reminded how certain simple foodstuffs can be made from other simple foodstuffs, especially if it's true that thousands of children don't even know where eggs come from.

Anyway, butter is basically heavy cream that has been agitated to the point where the fat globules destabilise and clump together, pushing out all the air and fluid. If you've got an electric whisk and a few spare minutes, this is another thing you and your children can do together and which they will fondly remember for ever afterwards, even if you only do it the once (see also bread and cheese making).

This works with 'heavy' cream, i.e. double or whipping cream, or a mixture of each, and you should get almost ½lb (225g) butter from one 300ml (10fl oz) carton of cream. You don't need to add anything at all, but the oil gives the butter a smoother texture and makes it more spreadable.

> **Makes 1lb (450g) butter**
> 2 cartons of heavy cream
> ½ teaspoon salt
> 1 tablespoon vegetable oil

1   Put the cream in a large mixing bowl (or use an electric mixer with the balloon whisk attachment) and beat the cream at medium-high speed for a couple of minutes until it's reached the stage where you'd normally stop mixing if you were whipping cream for dessert. Scrape the cream down from the sides of the bowl and carry on whisking.

2   In a few more seconds, the cream will start looking holey and too thick and this is quickly followed by the next stage, in which the cream looks like a very curdled cake mixture or dodgy scrambled egg (if you've ever seen scrambled eggs made with powdered egg, you'll know what I mean).

3   Keep whisking until the cream turns pale yellow and separates into solid butter and liquid buttermilk (there's no mistaking it).

4   Gently squeeze all the butter solids together into a lump with your hands. Run some cold water into the bowl to wash the butter and rinse the buttermilk away. This is an important part of the process as it stops the butter going rancid. You may need to do this a couple of times for larger amounts of butter. If you want to add salt and oil, put them in the bowl now and beat the butter again for another minute.

5   Shape the butter into a smooth block or roll. Wrap in greaseproof paper or keep covered in a china bowl in the fridge (or freeze). Use within three weeks.

Goats' Cheese

If you've never made soft cheese before, it's hard to believe that something as simple as this will work – but it does. Goats' cheese has a lovely fresh taste and a pleasing texture, but on its own it doesn't have an awful lot going for it, which is why it's best cooked and served with other, more flavoursome foods. Use it in much the same way as you'd use other types of soft cheese, i.e. drizzled with olive oil in salads, mixed into tomato-based pasta sauces or crumbled up with spinach and grated nutmeg on top of pizza. Finally, although you can make the cheese with around 6 tablespoons natural yoghurt (roughly 7fl oz/200ml or ½ a large carton) instead of lemon juice, adding another couple of tablespoons of yoghurt if the milk doesn't curdle quickly, I always use the lemon juice and it works every time.

Makes 12oz (350g) cheese
3½ pints (2 litres) full-fat goats' milk
2 tablespoons lemon juice OR 6 tablespoons plain natural yoghurt

1   Boil the milk in a large, heavy-based saucepan and while you're waiting, line a colander or large sieve with muslin or cheesecloth – or an old clean cotton tea towel if that's all you've got – and place over a large bowl or saucepan.
2   As soon as the milk boils and starts rising up the pan, add the lemon juice and stir gently until the milk curdles and separates, which should only take about a minute. If you're using yoghurt and the milk doesn't curdle after 1 minute, add another tablespoon.
3   Pour the contents of the pan into the lined sieve and run some cold water through it, then tie the cheese inside the cloth and tie the cloth to the tap over the sink to strain off the excess liquid.
4   After about 10 minutes, place the cheese on your work surface or kitchen table still wrapped in the cloth and put a heavy weight on top (use the same saucepan filled with the whey or water or the saucepan with a few tins or books inside).
5   In half an hour, the cheese will be flattened into a firm block. Wrap the goats' cheese in clingfilm and store in the fridge for up to two weeks.

Yoghurt

I twice tried making yoghurt with natural bio before my very good friend Carole pointed out that bio yoghurt is just plain yoghurt with added bacteria, and not the real thing – i.e. live yoghurt – which is what you need to start the yoghurt-making process. Now I know better.

I've used whole milk here, but you can make yoghurt with skimmed, semi-skimmed or evaporated milk, or a combination of any of these, with the addition of a little single cream for a deluxe result, and needless to say, you could use sheep or goats' milk if you wanted to.

You can also make yoghurt from a prepared culture of bacteria that can be bought online or in Lakeland, where you'll find do-it-yourself kits for making a variety of plain and flavoured yoghurts.

A very large saucepan (or a preserving pan), a sieve, a cloth and a couple of glass bowls are all you need, but an electric yoghurt maker is thermostatically controlled to keep the temperature constant while the yoghurt develops, so if you're serious about making yoghurt regularly, it may be worth getting one to avoid a duff result when your room was either too hot or too cold to do the job properly. If you want to make more yoghurt, remember to save a little from each batch to get the next one started.

> 2 pints (1.25 litres) whole milk
> 1 small (5oz/150g) pot of natural live yoghurt

1 Bring the milk to the boil in a very large saucepan, but not too quickly (if you burn the bottom of the pan, milk smells and tastes burnt all the way through).
2 Take the pan off the heat and strain into a scrupulously clean bowl through a sieve lined with a clean cloth. Let the milk cool down for about 15 minutes; you need it very warm, but you should be able to dip a finger into the milk without scalding it.

3 When the milk is at the right temperature, put the yoghurt into a second scrupulously clean glass or earthenware bowl. Stir a few tablespoons of warm milk into the yoghurt, then pour the rest of the milk into the bowl, stir well and cover with a plate or a thick cloth.

4 Leave the bowl in a warm room for a minimum of 8 hours, by which time the milk will have turned into yoghurt.

5 Transfer the yoghurt to clean containers with lids and refrigerate for up to one week.

For a high-energy breakfast, put 2 tablespoons yoghurt, 1 tablespoon muesli, 1 teaspoon each of hemp and flax seeds, 1 teaspoon runny honey, ½ teaspoon ground cinnamon and 1 small banana in a blender or food processor and whiz for a minute until smooth. Eat with a spoon.

Make smoothies and milkshakes with a couple of spoonfuls of yoghurt mixed with a combination of fresh (or tinned) fruit, ice cream syrups or juices and crushed ice.

Thicken soups and sauces with yoghurt, or a mixture of yoghurt and cream mixed with a little flour.

Replace some of the mayonnaise with yoghurt for lighter coleslaws and potato salads (see Eggs Mayonnaise Lite page 19)

Yorkshire Pudding

It's hard to be precise about quantities (see also gravy), but you won't go wrong with these.

For me, perfect Yorkshire pudding should be well risen, light, crisp and golden on top, and firm and a little bit stodgy on the bottom. Some people make the batter in advance and rest it in the fridge for a while, but I don't think it makes much difference. The most important factors are the flour, which should always be plain, the oil, which should be fizzing hot when the batter goes in, and the milk, which should be whole rather than semi-skimmed for best results.

Lastly, always use two eggs instead of just one, even for smaller quantities of batter. This gives it more substance and helps the pudding stay firm and well risen instead of collapsing and losing its shape a few seconds after you take it out of the oven.

The quantities below are enough for one family-sized Toad in the Hole or about 10 individual Yorkshire puddings, but as a rough guide, I'd say use 1 tablespoon flour per person and start with ¾ pint (425ml) milk, adding it gradually so you can see where you are before you've made the batter too thin and have to start sifting in more flour (in which case, it's better to sift more flour into another bowl, make a well in the centre, then pour in the too thin batter and gradually whisk the flour into that).

You need a very hot oven, 200–220C/400–425F/gas 6–7, and Yorkshire pudding takes approximately 10 to 20 minutes to cook, depending on whether you're making small, individual puddings or one very large one.

Makes 10 puddings
4oz (110g) plain flour
pinch of salt
2 eggs
½ pint (275ml) whole milk
oil

1 Sift the flour and salt into a large mixing bowl and make a well in the centre.

2 Break the eggs into the well one at a time, add a big splash of milk and start whisking with a fork or a small hand whisk, gradually adding more milk until you've got a fairly thick, smooth, pouring batter.

3 If you're making Toad in the Hole, wait until the sausages are brown and very nearly done, then quickly pour the batter directly into the oil and return to the top half of the oven immediately. After about 20 minutes you should have lovely dark brown sausages and perfect golden, well-risen Yorkshire pudding.

4 To make individual Yorkshire puddings, pour approximately 2 teaspoons oil into each of the holes in a Yorkshire pudding tin or large muffin tin. Put the tin in the preheated oven for about 10 minutes to really heat up the oil, then pour in enough batter to *almost* reach the top of each hole. Return to the oven as quickly as you can and check after 10 minutes.

Gravy

The quantities given in this recipe should be seen as a rough guide, and adapted according to how many people you're cooking for. If that sounds like a get-out clause, it's not meant to be. Making gravy from scratch is as easy as falling off a log and as long as you start with a joint of meat – beef or lamb are best – you really can't go wrong, believe me.

Place the meat directly on the vegetables if you want to or on a trivet of some kind – a wire cooling rack is ideal – so the meat juices drip down onto the vegetables underneath.

Soy sauce wasn't originally an ingredient of homemade gravy, obviously. Dr John Emsley of the Royal Society of Chemistry, an expert in these matters, said recently that it ought to be used instead of traditional gravy browning because the monosodium glutamate enhances the meaty flavour, which is why it's better to add a splash of soy sauce to any recipe where the meat is cooked in a large volume of liquid rather than overdose on the beef stock cubes (see the Steak and Ale Pie on page 129).

2 or 3 carrots
1 large leek or onion
sprigs of fresh rosemary and/or mixed herbs
salt & pepper
1 joint of meat, for roasting
1 level tablespoon gravy powder
1 level tablespoon plain flour
soy sauce or Worcestershire sauce

1   Wash and roughly chop the vegetables. Sprinkle with herbs, season with salt and pepper and mix everything up on the bottom of a large ovenproof roasting pan. Put the meat onto the bed of vegetables and cook in the usual way, or according to the instructions that come with the meat.

2   At the end of the meat's cooking time, prepare and cook vegetables – a mixture of cabbage or broccoli and carrots is ideal.

3   Remove the roasted meat and vegetables from the pan, leaving as much of the meat juices behind as you can. If you're worried there isn't enough liquid, pour a cupful of the vegetable water into the pan to loosen every trace of the meat deposits. Keep the vegetables covered in the fridge and boil them up later with some fresh peelings to make vegetable stock.

4   In a small bowl, blend the gravy powder and flour with a couple of tablespoons of cold water to make a smooth paste.

5   Put the pan over a gentle heat and stir the paste into the meat pan, then pour about ½ pint (275ml) vegetable water into the pan, still stirring. Add more vegetable water if you want more gravy, and thicken the gravy to the right consistency by turning the heat up and simmering to reduce the volume of liquid, stirring constantly.

6   Finish with a splash of soy sauce, Worcestershire sauce or a pinch of salt to serve.

Tortilla Baskets

Tortilla baskets add an extra dimension to salads. Not only do they look good and taste good, they have the magical effect of making the person who made them look good too.

All you need is a very large frying pan (unless you have a hotplate), a wire chip basket (8 inches/20cm approx), a sieve (6 inches/15cm approx) and a very large pan to fry the baskets in.

You can bake the tortillas in advance and make them into baskets later on (wrap in clingfilm to stop them drying out), but it's better to cook the baskets while the tortillas are warm and can be moulded more easily without cracking. Not only that, having one tortilla in the pan and one in the fryer speeds the whole process up. And if you want to make the baskets in advance, cover them with greaseproof paper and leave at room temperature for up to 24 hours before using. For ideas on what to put inside your tortilla baskets, see page 28.

Makes 6–8 tortilla baskets
½lb (225g) plain flour
1 level teaspoon baking powder
1 level teaspoon salt
4oz (110g) vegetable shortening, such as Trex
sunflower oil (2 litres plus)

1   Put the flour, baking powder and salt into a large bowl; add the fat in small pieces and rub in with your fingertips until the mixture resembles medium-fine breadcrumbs. Add roughly 7fl oz (200ml) cold water and use your hands to make a soft, elastic dough. Add another 2fl oz (55ml) water if the dough is on the dry side or a little more flour if it's too sticky (you'll know when it feels right).
2   Cover the bowl with a cloth and let the dough rest for about 20 minutes, then divide the dough into six to eight roughly same-sized pieces.
3   Meanwhile, in a very large pan warm enough oil to submerge the tortillas in the wire basket. Cover a couple of oven trays with

a layer of kitchen paper. Test the oil by dropping a small chunk of bread into the pan; if the bread turns golden in about half a minute, it's hot enough. Wipe out a large non-stick frying pan with a little oil and keep it warm over a low heat.

4   On a floured surface, roll out each piece of dough into a tortilla the size of a large dinner plate. Cook the tortillas in the frying pan for a minute on each side, turning the tortilla over once it starts to bubble and turn brown.

5   Press the warm tortilla into the wire basket; hold the basket in one hand and use your other hand to push the sieve down firmly on top of the tortilla. Plunge the whole thing into the hot oil and hold it there for about 2 minutes until the tortilla basket is crisp and a deep golden brown. Drain on the kitchen paper and repeat the process with each piece of dough.

Fish Fingers

The best fish fingers are made from pure fish fillets, as they are here. I usually make mine with haddock or a mixture of haddock, plaice, pollack, tuna and salmon. This helps spread the cost of the more expensive fish and makes things a bit more interesting since you won't know exactly what you've got until you cut the fish finger up on the plate.

Makes at least 20 big fish fingers
1½–2lb (700–900g) fresh white fish filets
2 eggs
a big splash of milk
4 tablespoons plain flour
salt & pepper
½lb (225g) fresh bread or cracker crumbs
oil

1   Wash the fish and blot dry with kitchen paper, then remove the skin and check for bones. Cut the fish up into thick strips, about 1½ inches (4cm) wide.

2   In a small bowl, beat the eggs with a big splash of milk and put the seasoned flour on a dinner plate. Make breadcrumbs by whizzing the bread or crackers in the food processor in the usual way, then spread them out on a tray.

3   Meanwhile, warm just enough oil in a very large pan to cover the fish fingers and preheat the oven to 190c/375F/gas 5.

4   Dust the fish strips with the seasoned flour, then dip into the beaten egg mixture and coat in breadcrumbs.

5   When all the fish fingers are ready, deep fry in large batches for about 3 minutes, then put them on an oven tray and cook for a further 5 to 10 minutes.

Pasta

You don't actually need a pasta-making machine to make your own, but one would be helpful at Step 6 when your arms are aching from trying to roll out the dough and it just doesn't want to go. After that though, the process does get easier, so just grit your teeth for a couple of minutes and wait for the moment to pass.

Unless you're already adept at handling fresh pasta, in which case you probably have a machine anyway, by far the best thing is to make ravioli, which can be filled with any number of meaty or tomato-based sauces and cheese. Each ravioli parcel only takes a teaspoon of filling, so it's ideal for using up small amounts of leftover Bolognese sauce, flaked tuna in cheese sauce, feta cheese and ham, mushroom and red onion or tomato and garlic purée mixed with grated cheese. Grate or crumble the cheese finely, chop all the ingredients into small pieces and cook first in a little butter to soften.

Whether you're using ordinary plain flour or superfine oo flour, be sure to sift it twice before you start and don't get too heavy-handed in the early stages when you're mixing the eggs into the flour. You won't need all the flour, so it's important not to shovel too much into the mixture at Step 3; if you do, the pasta will be ruined and, unfortunately, this is one of those mistakes that you just can't put right.

Finally, the amounts given here are enough for about eight servings, so you could store half the dough in the fridge for a couple of days, then when you're ready to use the pasta, let it rest at room temperature for at least two hours and knead it gently for a few minutes before rolling it out again.

Makes enough for 8
3 full mugs of flour (00 or plain) (about 1½lb/700g)
4 large eggs
salt
oil

1   Sift the flour twice and make a big pile on a clean work surface or a very large wooden board. Make a deep well in the centre. Break the eggs into the well one at a time and use a blunt dinner knife to gently work the flour in a little at a time, taking care not to send the liquid cascading over the edge of the flour and all over the worktop.

2   Once you've added all the eggs and mixed in enough flour to get a soft dough, gather the remaining flour together and sift it back onto your work surface in a neat pile so you're working with clean, new flour again. This whole stage takes around 5 minutes.

3   Re-flour your work surface and knead the dough for about 15 minutes, adding a little more flour as and when you need it to stop it becoming too sticky, and pushing the dough away from you with the heels of your hands. Little by little the dough becomes increasingly pliable and springy, until pressing it with your finger makes a dent, which quickly disappears, meaning the dough is ready.

4   Wrap the dough in clingfilm or cover it with an upturned bowl and allow it to rest for 20 to 30 minutes at room temperature.

5 Roll the dough out with a large rolling pin, turning frequently and adding a little more flour when necessary, until the dough is as thin as you can get it without breaking and you can see the shadow of your hand through it.

6 Use a large pastry cutter with a fluted edge – or an ordinary mug if you don't have one – to cut out as many rounds as you can. Put the pasta rounds on a lightly floured tray while you re-roll the trimmings, lightly kneading the dough a bit more each time to keep it malleable without overworking it.

7 Put a teaspoon of filling (see above) onto the centre of each piece of pasta and fold the rounds into semi-circles, pressing the edges together to seal the ravioli. Don't try and use water to help seal the edges as you would with pastry, this makes the pasta too tacky without actually sticking it together for some reason.

8 Cook the ravioli in a large saucepan of salted boiling water for about 3 minutes and serve with grated fresh Parmesan cheese and salad.

9 To store in the fridge, dust the ravioli with a little flour and put it in a large food bag or on a plate covered with clingfilm.

Pastry

Apart from filo and puff, pastry is very easy to make. All you need is a few minutes, cold hands and something to roll the dough out with: a rolling pin if you've got one, but an empty straight-sided wine bottle is perfect if you don't. The ratio of flour to fat for everyday pastry is almost always two to one and once you've made it a few times, you'll know what the quantities look like and be able to measure the ingredients accurately enough without using the scales.

Cooking times vary slightly according to the recipe, but most types of pastry generally cook in around 25 to 30 minutes in a hot oven on 190–200C/375–400F/gas 5–6, except filo pastry, which cooks more quickly, being much less substantial than the rest. In any case, pastry is obviously cooked when it's crisp and golden or if it's been baked blind, when it's clearly dry and a pale beige colour, as opposed to looking wet and raw.

Shortcrust Pastry

The most basic type of pastry, this is all you'll ever need for the majority of everyday pies and flans, savoury or sweet. You don't have to include lard or Trex, but they both give the pastry a melt-in-the-mouth quality that you won't get with butter or margarine alone.

> **Makes enough pastry to easily line a shallow, loose-bottomed 8–9 inch (20–23cm) flan tin**
> 8oz (225g) plain flour
> 2oz (50g) butter or margarine
> 2oz (50g) lard or Trex
> 4 tablespoons cold water or milk (approx)

1   Sift the flour into a very large mixing bowl and rub in the fat in small pieces until the mixture resembles medium-fine breadcrumbs.

2   Make a well in the centre, then add the water or milk, gradually incorporating the flour by pinching the mixture together with the fingers of one hand. Knead the pastry inside the bowl for a minute to make a firm, smooth dough.
3   Wrap the dough in foil or clingfilm and chill in the fridge for half an hour before turning the dough onto a floured surface and rolling it out to fit a lightly greased flan tin or pie dish.
4   Prick the pastry with a fork several times before adding the filling. If the pastry case is to be baked 'blind' – i.e. on its own so the filling can be added when the pastry is cold – cover with a circle of greaseproof paper, then weigh the paper down with a handful of dried beans, lentils or rice. Preheat the oven to 180C/350F/gas 4.
5   Bake for 10 to 15 minutes. Remove the dried beans and greaseproof paper and return to the oven for a further 5 minutes to crisp the pastry.

Sweet Pastry

This is sometimes called pâte sucrée, but again, it's only a very slight variation of the basic recipe and just as easy to make.

Makes enough pastry to line an 8–9 inch (20–23cm) flan tin
8oz (225g) plain flour
5oz (150g) butter or margarine
2oz (50g) caster sugar
1 egg

1   Sift the flour into a large mixing bowl and rub in the butter or margarine in small pieces until the mixture resembles medium-fine breadcrumbs.
2   Make a well in the centre of the mixture and add the sugar and beaten egg.
3   Using a metal spoon, gradually incorporate the liquid into the mixture, lightly mixing to a smooth paste, and finish by kneading

the dough with your hands for a couple of minutes on a floured surface.

4 Wrap and allow to rest in a cool place for about half an hour before use.

Orange Pastry

This is especially good for making mince pies and you should get about 24 from this amount of pastry. It is also good for making the Cherry and Chicory Pie on page 62.

> **Makes enough pastry to line an 8–9 inch (20–23cm) flan tin**
> zest and juice of 1 large orange
> 8oz (225g) flour
> 3oz (75g) butter or margarine
> 1oz (25g) lard or Trex

1 Wash the orange with warm water and a nailbrush, then finely grate the rind into a small bowl. Cut the orange into two halves and squeeze all the juice into the bowl.

2 Sift the flour into a large mixing bowl and rub in the fat in small pieces until the mixture resembles medium-fine breadcrumbs.

3 Add the grated rind and juice of the orange to the bowl and pinch the mixture together with your fingertips to make a fairly soft dough. If the mixture is still too dry, add a little cold water or a few drops from a carton of orange juice.

4 Wrap and rest in the fridge for about half an hour before use.

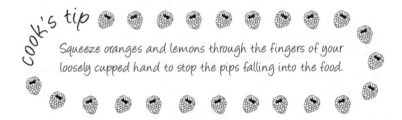

cook's tip
Squeeze oranges and lemons through the fingers of your loosely cupped hand to stop the pips falling into the food.

Suet Crust

Suet has got a bit of a bad name, most unfairly really, because it contains less saturated fat than butter. If you can buy fresh suet from your butcher he'll probably be able to shred it for you too, otherwise Atora make good dried suet, which keeps in the cupboard for a couple of months.

This pastry can either be baked in the same way as shortcrust for sausage rolls and pies, or steamed, say for steak and kidney pudding.

> 8oz (225g) self-raising flour
> pinch of salt
> 4oz (110g) suet

1 Sift the flour and salt into a large bowl and mix well with the suet. Make a well in the centre.
2 Pour about 4fl oz (120ml) water into the well and use your hand to pinch the mixture together to make a fairly stiff dough, gradually adding more water if you need it.
3 Roll out the dough on a floured surface. Use straight away or keep it covered at room temperature until you need it.

Rough Puff Pastry

Making proper puff pastry that isn't rough requires more skill and patience than I think I've got, but this simplified version isn't anywhere near as daunting. In fact, the rolling and folding process is so addictive I usually find myself doing a few extra turns each time, rather than rushing to get it over with.

You can use ordinary plain flour, but strong bread flour helps to support the extra fat in the dough so it's not too soft and unworkable.

8oz (225g) strong bread flour
pinch of salt
6oz (175g) butter or margarine
splash of lemon juice

1   Sieve the flour and salt into a large mixing bowl and cut the fat
    into tiny pieces, straight from the fridge, so it's as cold and hard
    as possible. Don't rub in the fat, but lightly mix it in with the flour,
    then make a well in the centre.

2   Add just under ½ pint (150ml) ice-cold water and the lemon juice
    to the well and pinch the mixture together with your fingertips,
    gradually adding the rest of the water to make a fairly stiff dough.

3   Turn the dough onto a floured surface and roll it into a roughly
    12 x 4 inch (30 x 10cm) rectangle, using your hands to keep all the
    sides as straight and even as possible.

4   Fold a third of the pastry into the middle from one end, then fold
    the other third over from the opposite end to make a square with
    three layers.

5   Make a quarter turn to the left so the layered edges of the pastry
    square are at the top and bottom, then roll the pastry out to a
    rectangle again, the same size as before, still taking care to keep
    the sides straight. Repeat the process two or three times, making
    a quarter turn to the left each time, then cover the pastry with
    a clean cloth and leave it to rest where it is for about 15 minutes.

6   Repeat Step 5 twice more, with a second 15 minute break in
    between. The pastry is now ready to be rolled out and used.

Potato Pastry

The addition of cold mashed potatoes gives ordinary shortcrust
pastry a bit of extra oomph. If you do make the mash for your pastry
from scratch, don't add butter and milk to the cooked potatoes or
you'll need to shovel in a lot more flour to make the dough workable.
Potato pastry also makes a good pizza base.

6oz (175g) plain flour

1oz (25g) butter or margarine

1oz (25g) lard or Trex

8oz (225g) cold mashed potato (approx)

2–3 tablespoons milk

1   Sift the flour into a large mixing bowl and rub in the fat in small pieces until the mixture resembles medium-fine breadcrumbs.

2   Add the mash to the bowl and squish it into the mixture with your hands, adding a few drops of milk if necessary – go carefully, you may not need any at all – to make a fairly soft, but workable dough.

3   Wrap and rest the dough in the fridge for about half an hour. Roll out on a floured surface in the usual way.

Mincemeat

Mincemeat made with meat is a very old recipe that fell out of fashion not long after Mrs Beeton's time, but which now seems to be enjoying a bit of a renaissance.

These quantities are enough to fill a large jam jar, which is more than enough if you only want to make a couple of dozen mince pies to see you through Christmas, otherwise increase the amount of everything by three or four to make enough mincemeat to last the whole winter. Believe it or not, it really does keep that long.

Makes a large jar
½lb (225g) mixed dried fruit and peel (approx)
4oz (110g) lean beef steak
1 orange
1 lemon
4oz (110g) brown sugar
4oz (110g) beef suet
1 level teaspoon nutmeg
1 large Bramley cooking apple (½lb/225g)
1 full liqueur glass (2fl oz/55ml) brandy

1   Wash the mixed fruit and peel in warm water and dry thoroughly, either in an old clean tea towel or on a tray at the bottom of the oven on the lowest setting for a few minutes. Let it cool completely before you put it in the bowl at Step 3.
2   Mince the raw lean beef or cut it into tiny pieces with kitchen scissors, then put it on a board and chop more finely with a very sharp knife.
3   Put the beef in a mixing bowl. Finely grate the orange and lemon zest over the meat, then add the sugar, suet and nutmeg to the bowl in that order. Put the mixed fruit and peel on top and leave to stand without mixing while you prepare the apple.
4   Peel and finely chop the apple, then add to the bowl; sprinkle the brandy over the top and thoroughly squish everything together.

5   Meanwhile, sterilise a large jam jar and cut out a circle of
    greaseproof paper the same size as the lid.
6   Pack the mincemeat into the jar, pressing it down gently as you
    go to eliminate any air pockets, put the greaseproof paper on the
    top, seal with the lid, label and leave for two to three weeks in a
    cool, dark cupboard before using.

Mincemeat Pies

These mince pies – in fact any mince pies – are especially good with the orange pastry in this chapter, or make them with shortcrust or sweet pastry if you prefer.

Makes 24 mince pies (approx)
1lb (45g) shortcrust, sweet or orange pastry (see page 152)
milk, for glazing
½lb (225g) mincemeat (see page 156)

1 Preheat the oven to 190C/375F/gas 5 and lightly grease two cup cake tins with butter.
2 On a lightly floured surface, roll out the pastry to about 3mm; cut out as many circles as you can with a large pastry cutter – or a mug if you don't have one – and put the rounds in the cup cake tins.
3 Prick the pastry rounds with a fork, brush the outside edges of the pastry with milk and put a dessertspoonful of mincemeat in the centre.
4 Put a second pastry circle on top of each one to make a lid, pinching the edges together between your finger and thumb, and use a pastry brush to glaze the pies with milk.
5 Re-roll the trimmings, keeping any unused pastry in the fridge to use again once the first lot of pies are done.

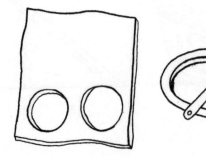

And in your Good Life
extreme dreams . . .

Keeping Chickens

More and more people are keeping chickens these days, so if you don't live in a very big house in the country, there's a company called Omlet (Omelet.co.uk) who make plastic hen houses, or Eglus, designed for smaller gardens and home assembly.

All the chickens really need apart from food, water and shelter is enough room to roam a bit and plenty of grit to peck at (for making good shells), then they should be happy little hens who'll lay pretty much continually for a couple of years. It takes from around £300 to get started, but the chickens themselves cost about £10, which is roughly what you'd pay for a large, organic free-range chicken in the supermarket when you think about it.

The hen keepers I know all swear their chickens have personalities, usually good ones, although I've heard a story about a lesbian hen who thinks she's a rooster and whose future is hanging in the balance since she bullied one of the other hens in the group to the point where the poor little thing now lives apart from the rest. And unfortunately, pot-roasted chicken isn't the answer either. They have to be eaten when they're a few months old, so if you thought you could love your chickens for a couple of years and eat them once they've stopped laying, forget it.

The quality of the eggs is noticeably better than anything you find in the supermarket and if you keep a couple of chickens, you'll have more than enough eggs to share with your family and friends, which is a huge bonus for those of us who live in an urban wasteland, with nothing in our own gardens except a trampoline and the wheelie bin.

Keeping Bees

If keeping chickens is a pipe dream, making my own honey is a few fantasies further down the line – somewhere between highly unlikely and never gonna happen – although obviously you don't 'make your own' honey, the bees do it for you. (Even if you have about as much chance of keeping bees as flying to the moon, it's fun to think about these things sometimes.)

Beginners are advised to start small and not be tempted to expand too quickly for obvious reasons. But even a couple of hives greatly increases pollination and productivity in your garden. And if you'd love to keep bees but don't have nerves of steel, remember August Boatwright's advice in the novel *The Secret Life of Bees*, which is to approach the bees with love. That way there's no room to be frightened.

Just imagine having your own supply of organic honey (20–30lb/9–14kg per year is a rough average) and all the things you could do with it. Apart from being a tastier and healthier substitute for refined sugar with everything from porridge to stewed fruit, honey has antibacterial properties, which make it an excellent sore throat remedy, and it can also be used as an ingredient in some cocktails and in cooking. Simple soaps, cosmetics, candles and furniture polish can all be made from the beeswax.

Further information from:
The British Beekeeping Association www.britishbee.org.uk
Fiona Nevile at The Cottage Smallholder website
www.cottagesmallholder.com.

Making Your Own Sausages

You can make sausages at home with the most basic equipment, but if you want to make them regularly you might want to invest in a sausage machine. Manual sausage makers cost around £40, the electrical ones are more than double that, or you can use an ordinary plastic funnel to fit the skins onto and feed the meat mixture through.

Sausage skins can be dried natural collagen casings (ordered online) or pork caul fat from the butcher, cut into squares and wrapped around the meat mixture.

Being able to choose exactly what type of meat, and how much, is one of the great advantages of making your own sausages. The best shop-bought sausages contain upwards of 70% meat, but when you make your own, you have more control. In fact, you could make the sausages with 100% meat, but the right filler actually improves the succulence of the sausage by absorbing some of the meat juices, so it's better to make your sausages with a combination of lean and fatty meat and 10 to 15% filler – ideally fresh white breadcrumbs or cracker crumbs.

Sage, rosemary, chives, mixed herbs, ginger, ground cloves, cayenne pepper, horseradish, mustard, dried apricots and cranberries, cooked apple and onion can all be mixed with the meat. The best thing is to make a small amount of your chosen flavour to start with, then cook and taste a little of the mixture before committing yourself to a dozen or more sausages.

Expert sausage makers say they should be cooked slowly, which is hard to get used to if you normally whack the oven up to 200c/400f/gas 6 and cook them in 30 minutes flat. Don't preheat the oven and cook your homemade sausages on 170c/325f/gas 3 for about 1 hour. That way, the moisture in the sausages steams gently and cooks the meat without drying it out or causing the skins to break. Further information from designasausage.com.

Brewing Your Own Beer

Home brewing is a highly complex business, but the basics are easy enough to get to grips with and endlessly fascinating, so much so that if I actually liked beer, I'd be very tempted to make it again. The one and only time I did make it, it was drinkable and there were no explosions in the bottles, so I considered it a success.

Makes roughly 8 (beer) bottles
1oz (25g) hops
1lb (450g) liquid malt extract
½oz (12g) dried yeast
sugar cubes

1   Put the hops and malt in a very large, heavy-bottomed pan with 8 pints (3.75 litres) cold water and bring to the boil. Boil steadily without a lid on for about 1½ hours, stirring occasionally.
2   Take the pan off the heat and replace however much liquid you've lost – probably about 2 pints (1.25 litres) – with roughly the same amount of cold water. Stir and leave to cool for about 1 hour.
3   When the liquid is lukewarm, strain through an old clean tea towel into a sterilised plastic bucket with a tight-fitting lid, then sprinkle on the dried yeast, stir, cover and leave to stand at room temperature for three days.
4   Siphon the beer into sterilised bottles with screw caps, leaving at least 1 inch (2.5cm) of room at the top. Put two to three sugar lumps per pint in each bottle and replace the caps loosely, i.e. not screwed on. Leave for two weeks. After that, the beer will be ready to drink.

Further information from Brewmart, thebrewmart.com and *Home Brewing* by John Parkes (New Holland).

Hostess with the mostest

'1. Party girl and social butterfly (although not ladette). Often nocturnal, but can also be early riser on high days and holidays.'

Anyone can be a good hostess. All you really need is a sense of humour and enough enthusiasm for having the party in the first place. It doesn't matter if you cook like an angel and know how to turn a paper napkin into the Sydney Opera House. If you try too hard and expect too much of yourself, you'll end up feeling peeved and unappreciated, and your party won't be a success.

Someone I knew when my children were small couldn't cook to save her life and served everything straight from the packet, but she did it with such exuberance – and so much sparkling wine, it must be said – nobody cared that her birthday cakes looked and tasted like a piece of road kill smothered in Jelly Tots.

But luckily, you don't have to be a cordon bleu cook or a master baker to produce good party food, so unless you're used to catering for large numbers of people, don't be overly ambitious and stray too far from your comfort zone. Just know

what you want and what you think your guests will like
and you're already halfway there.

Kidult Parties

When they're older, your children's memories of their birthday parties will merge into a kaleidoscope of bouncy castles, balloon sculptures and musical chairs, with a vague recollection of falling off things and occasionally throwing up. What they definitely won't remember is that you made green and orange jelly eggs with little aliens inside for Halloween and knew how to turn a cucumber into a crocodile. It's a different story with the mothers, however, and if there's one thing women love more at a party than somebody else's child behaving really badly and making a show of them, it's a great selection of chips and dips followed by a nice bit of cake.

Keep it simple, but not as simple as a woman I won't name, who once threw a children's party on a few jam sandwiches, a couple of bags of crisps and a shop-bought birthday cake that she didn't even cut. To add insult to injury, she said there was no food for the adults (as if we hadn't noticed) and failed to make anyone a cup of tea.

And to prove that you can still be a hostess with the mostest in truly dire circumstances, someone I will name – my sister-in-law Claire – had a lovely party with home-cooked finger food for my niece, Charlotte, a few days after moving house and a few hours after a pipe burst, bringing down the dining room ceiling, and she was nine months pregnant at the time.

Cheese and Fruit Crocodile

I learnt this trick many years ago when I was still a new mum,
as opposed to quite an old one. The girl who showed me how to
do it was called Sarah and she had two little boys, which is the only
thing I remember now all I have left of those days is a photo album
full of the ghosts of mums and toddlers past, and fond memories
of parties where only the parents drank the alcohol.

Anyway, the beauty of this recipe, if you can call it that, is that
there's no cooking involved and even though it looks really good,
it's so astonishingly simple the children could probably make it
themselves.

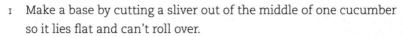

2 whole cucumbers
1 long red or deep pink balloon
2 green olives stuffed with red pimento
tinned pineapple
cheese
cocktail sticks

1   Make a base by cutting a sliver out of the middle of one cucumber
     so it lies flat and can't roll over.
2   At the end of the cucumber that looks most like a crocodile's snout,
     i.e. not the rounded end, cut away any remaining bit of stalk, then
     use a very sharp, small knife to make a zig-zig pattern about
     4 inches (10cm) in length from the tip of the cucumber, making
     sure the knife goes all the way through.
3   Turn the cucumber over and do the same thing on the other side.
     When you've finished, the two halves of the cucumber should
     spring apart to look like a crocodile's open jaws.
4   Place the balloon inside the mouth to look like a tongue and give
     the crocodile two bulging eyes by using a piece of cocktail stick
     to secure half a stuffed olive on either side of his head. Push the
     sticks in far enough so they don't show. Use a black permanent
     marker pen to draw the nostrils.

5   Cut two chunks, approximately 2 inches (5cm) thick from the wide part of the second cucumber and cut each chunk in half lengthways to make four semi-circular chunks. Use more cocktail sticks to hold the chunks in place on either side of the crocodile where his feet should be.

6   Cut the fruit and cheese into roughly same-sized cubes, spear on cocktail sticks and place in rows along the crocodile's body.

cook's tip

For variety and lots of extra colour, alternate rows of Cheddar cheese and pineapple with feta cheese and black olives, Cheshire cheese and raspberries, blue cheese and peaches or fresh fruit without the cheese. Strawberries, blueberries and cherries (without the stones) are also good.

Cheese Twists

These are a slightly more sophisticated version of the cheese straws your mum and granny used to make back in the seventies, so we're moving onwards and upwards (but not that much).

The quantities below make around 24 to 30 twists, depending upon how much pastry is wasted in the process, although if you're really good at rolling out ready-made pastry, you may not make any waste at all. Alternatively, once you've made the first lot of twists you could use the trimmings to make biscuits for the kids by pressing out different shapes with a set of children's pastry cutters.

Makes 24 to 30 twists
1 packet (375g/13oz) ready-made puff pastry

1 large egg yolk
2–3 tablespoons single cream
2oz (50g) Cheddar cheese
1oz (25g) Parmesan cheese
1 tablespoon paprika

1 Preheat the oven to 200C/400F/gas 6. Roll out the pastry on
a floured surface and trim the edges to make a neat rectangle.
In one small bowl, mix the beaten egg yolk with the cream.
In another, mix the finely grated cheeses with the paprika.
2 Brush the pastry with the egg wash and cover with the cheese
mixture.
3 Cut the pastry in half lengthways and mark each half into strips
roughly ¾ inch (2cm) thick.
4 Pinch the pastry strips between forefinger and thumb at each end
and twist in opposite directions two or three times.
5 Put the cheese twists on well-oiled baking trays and brush with
more egg wash. Bake for about 10 minutes until the pastry is crisp
and golden.

cook's tip

Sprinkle the pastry with sesame seeds, poppy seeds,
crushed pumpkin seeds or a mixture of all three instead
of cheese and paprika.

Chips and Dips

Tortilla Chips

Buy ready-made tortillas and make them into chips at home. That way, you can cut them into various shapes and sizes and play around with the seasoning to suit yourself. Make them even better value for money by buying bigger, economy packets of the supermarket's own brand.

> 2 packets (16) tortilla wraps
> olive oil
> salt
> *Customise by sprinkling with*
> grated Parmesan cheese
> black pepper
> 1 teaspoon paprika
> 1 teaspoon cayenne pepper
> garlic salt
> lime zest

1 Preheat the oven to 200C/400F/gas 6.
2 Very lightly grease two or three baking trays and place one tortilla wrap on one of the trays.
3 Brush the surface of the tortilla with olive oil and one of the seasonings or just a little salt (mix the seasoning with the oil or sprinkle separately, it's up to you). Place another tortilla on top, brush the surface of that one with olive oil and repeat with the rest of the tortillas until they're stacked up on the tray.
4 Cut the tortillas in half and cut each half into three or four triangles, according to how big you want the chips to be.
5 Place flat on the trays without overlapping and bake for 5 to 10 minutes until the tortilla chips are crisp and just golden. It's hard to say exactly how long the chips take to cook, but it's only

a matter of minutes and they go from perfect to burnt in a very short time, so check after 5 minutes, keep your eye on them and don't go off and do something else.

cook's tip

Use either the corn or flour variety of tortilla, or a mixture of each.

Dips

The quantities given here for each dip will fill a small bowl or large ramekin.

Avocado Dip

I wouldn't call this avocado dip 'guacamole' (I have before and been corrected), but it's very similar, so if you like one, you'll like the other. Swap the yoghurt for mayonnaise for even less authenticity and a creamier texture.

> 1 large avocado
> 1 tablespoon finely chopped tomato
> ¼ teaspoon chilli powder
> 1 clove of garlic, crushed
> 1 tablespoon Greek yoghurt or mayonnaise
> splash of lemon juice
> black pepper

1   Mash the avocado in a bowl, add the rest of the ingredients and mix well. Cover with a layer of clingfilm and keep refrigerated for up to 2 days.

Garlic and Cheese Dip

For best results, the cheese should be finely grated.

> 4oz (110g) extra mature Cheddar cheese
> 2–3 cloves of garlic
> 2 tablespoons mayonnaise
> 1 tablespoon natural yoghurt
> chives
> parsley
> salt

1 Finely grate the cheese and add the crushed garlic, mayonnaise, yoghurt and herbs – fresh and finely chopped or dried – according to taste.
2 Season with a little salt, cover and refrigerate.

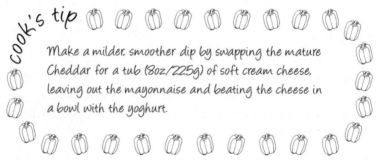

cook's tip

Make a milder, smoother dip by swapping the mature Cheddar for a tub (8oz/225g) of soft cream cheese, leaving out the mayonnaise and beating the cheese in a bowl with the yoghurt.

Tzatziki

Although I use dried herbs more often than fresh, at least for everyday cooking, this is one of those recipes where it does make a difference, so use fresh mint if you possibly can.

> ½ smallish cucumber (approx)
> 1–2 tablespoons olive oil
> 2 cloves of garlic

¼ teaspoon salt
1 small carton of Greek yoghurt
1 small handful of fresh mint

1 Peel and chop the cucumber, slicing it thinly and finely dicing the slices. Deseed it as well if you've got the patience.
2 In a bowl, mix the olive oil with the crushed garlic and salt, then stir in the yoghurt.
3 Add the finely chopped cucumber and mint, stir well, then cover with clingfilm and chill in the fridge. Serve garnished with black olives and a sprig of fresh mint.

Salsa

There are lots of variations of this recipe and this is just the way I make it, so if it isn't classic, I apologise. Use good-quality tomatoes: home grown, or deep red, vine-ripened from the supermarket.

For a hotter salsa, add a splash of Tabasco or more jalapeños. For a tangier flavour, add the finely grated zest of half a lime and a good squeeze of juice.

4 tomatoes
2 red jalapeños
1 red onion
1 large clove of garlic
1 tablespoon extra virgin olive oil
1 tablespoon red wine vinegar
coriander
salt & pepper

1 Chop and deseed the tomatoes and jalapeños. Finely chop the red onion and crush the garlic.
2 Mix the tomato, jalapeños, onion and garlic in a bowl with the olive oil, vinegar and finely chopped coriander, according to taste. Season with salt and pepper, cover and keep in the fridge.

Falafel

Normally you need to start with raw chickpeas to make falafel, but the addition of porridge oats automatically makes this another 'wrong' recipe, so you may as well use the tinned variety, which makes the whole thing quicker and easier still.

Makes 18–20
1 tin of chickpeas
2 tablespoons rolled (porridge) oats
2 teaspoons curry powder
1 teaspoon ground cumin
1 teaspoon dried parsley
½ teaspoon dried coriander
salt
1oz (25g) melted butter
plain or gram flour
oil

1   Drain the tin and mash the chickpeas in a bowl.
2   Add the porridge oats, spices, herbs, salt and melted butter and bind the whole lot together with the back of the tablespoon, a fork or your hand to make a thick paste.
3   Sift a couple of tablespoons of plain or gram flour, or a mixture of each, on to a dinner plate. Roll the mixture into balls roughly the size of a large marble and dust with plenty of flour.
4   In a large pan, warm just enough oil to cover the falafel and as soon as the oil is hot enough (test with a cube of stale bread – it should turn brown in under a minute) deep fry for 1 to 2 minutes until golden.
5   Drain on kitchen paper and store in the fridge for up to one week.

Lemony Chicken Nuggets

Most kids love chicken nuggets, as do most adults, even if they
don't want to admit to it. I often mix ready-made stuffing with
minced meat because it makes the meat go further as well as
improving the texture, which can be especially helpful if you're
feeding a fussy little eater or two, and the addition of the sage and
onion with lots of lemon also boosts the flavour of these chicken
nuggets (use another type of stuffing if you like). Now my children
are older, I make bigger chicken nuggets, but assuming you want
a regular size, the quantities here will easily make thirty-six,
if not more.

Makes at least 36
1 small sachet of stuffing mix
4 chicken fillets
zest and juice of 2 large lemons
4 big tablespoons plain flour
2 eggs
splash of milk
½lb (225g) fresh white breadcrumbs (or cracker crumbs)
oil

1 Make up the stuffing mix according to the instructions on the
   packet and let it cool completely before you combine it with
   the chicken.
2 Remove the chicken skin, trim off any little fatty bits and mince
   the meat, either in a mincer or by pulsing in a food processor to
   make a sort of rough paste with a chunky texture.
3 Put the chicken in a large bowl with as much of the stuffing mix
   as you want to use. Packet sizes vary and you may find you want
   less stuffing than you've made, which is why it's a good idea to add
   the lemon last, when you're completely happy with the mixture.
4 Finely grate the whole lemons into a small bowl, then cut them
   in half and squeeze all the juice into the bowl. Get rid of the pips

and mix the lemon into the chicken and stuffing mixture. Squish everything together with your hands.

5 Put the flour on a dinner plate, shape the nuggets with your hands and coat in the flour. Chill the chicken nuggets in the fridge for about half an hour (cold nuggets are easier to handle). Meanwhile, beat the eggs in a small bowl with a big splash of milk and spread the breadcrumbs out on a large tray.

6 Dip each chicken nugget into the egg mixture, then coat in breadcrumbs. Work with a small amount of breadcrumbs at a time to avoid making a mess of the whole tray and creating too much waste.

7 Warm enough oil in a very large pan to completely cover the nuggets and test if it's hot enough by dropping a small chunk of bread into the pan – it should go brown in about a minute. Preheat the oven to 200C/400F/gas 6.

8 Fry the nuggets in batches for a couple of minutes until they're lightly golden on the outside, then finish them off on a tray in the oven for between 10 to 20 minutes to cook through. To serve cold, let the cooked nuggets cool down on kitchen paper, then get them into the fridge as soon as possible.

cook's tip

- Instead of using a ready-made stuffing mix, make your own with a combination of fresh white breadcrumbs, finely chopped herbs (parsley and sage are good), plus lemon juice and zest.
- You can also make chicken nuggets by mixing the minced meat with grated apple, carrot and onion.

Piglets in Blankets

These are a great alternative to regular sausage rolls, warm or cold.
If you're making them mainly for adults or older kids, spice them
up a bit by spreading the ham with French or English mustard before
rolling round the sausages.

If you're very good at rolling ready-made pastry into one
perfect rectangle on the first go, mark the pastry into 24 squares
(6 × 4), otherwise cut off the rough edges of the pastry and mark
into 20 squares, re-rolling the trimmings to make the rest. Or make
it even easier on yourself by using ready rolled ready-made pastry.

Makes 24
12 chipolatas
1 × ½lb (225g) packet of ham (square) slices
1 packet (375g/13oz) ready-made puff pastry
4–5 tablespoons milk

1   Preheat the oven to 200–220C/400–425F/gas 6–7 and liberally oil
    a large baking tray.
2   Gently squeeze the chipolatas in the middle until you're down
    to the skin, then twist the two halves in opposite directions and
    separate with kitchen scissors to make two cocktail sausages.
3   Cut the ham squares in half and wrap each little sausage in one
    piece of ham.
4   On a floured surface, roll out the pastry into a large rectangle, cut
    in half lengthways, then cut each half into small squares, slightly
    longer than the sausages.
5   Brush the pastry squares all over with milk, put a sausage wrapped
    in ham on each one, then roll up and pinch the pastry together at
    each end.
6   Put the sausage rolls on the prepared baking tray, join side down,
    and brush with more milk. Bake for 12 to 15 minutes until the
    pastry is a deep golden brown.

Pizza Men

My gingerbread man cutter is 4½ inches (12cm) long, which makes about 18 pizza men from the quantities below.

Makes 18

½lb (225g) self-raising flour
2 teaspoons baking powder
2oz (50g) grated Cheddar cheese
2oz (50g) butter
1 large egg
2 tablespoons milk
olive oil

For the toppings

tomato purée
mozzarella
ham
pineapple

1 Grease two large baking trays with oil. Preheat the oven to 200C/400F/gas 6.
2 Sift the flour and baking powder into a large bowl and mix in half the grated cheese. Make a well in the centre.
3 Put the melted butter, beaten egg and milk into the well. Mix together with a fork to start with, then pinch the mixture together with your fingertips to make a smooth, fairly stiff dough.
4 On a floured surface, roll out the dough to a thickness of about 3mm and cut into shapes with the gingerbread man cutter, re-rolling the trimmings as you go. Put the dough men on the greased baking trays, brush with olive oil and cover with clingfilm while you prepare the toppings.
5 Squeeze a teaspoonful of tomato purée onto each man and use the back of the teaspoon to spread the paste over the dough up to 5mm from the edge all the way round.
6 Mix the remaining 1oz (25g) of Cheddar with roughly the same amount of mozzarella. Cut the ham and pineapple (or whatever else you're using) into very small pieces, put the toppings on the pizza men, sprinkle with grated cheese and bake for about 12 minutes or until the dough is crisp and golden and the cheese is bubbling.

Mars Bar Krispie Cakes

I'd heard you can make chocolate krispie cakes with melted Mars bars, but hadn't tried it until now.

The nougat and caramel in the Mars bars give the cakes a nice gooey squidginess, but you do have to add a certain amount of straight chocolate to the mix to get the texture right and stop the Mars bars welding themselves into a giant sticky ball.

Makes 18 (approx)
4 Mars bars
4oz (110g) milk or plain chocolate
3 mugfuls rice krispies (approx)

1. Break up the Mars bars and chocolate in a large bowl and melt over a saucepan of boiling water, stirring frequently and breaking up the Mars bars with a metal spoon. (The mixture will still be fairly lumpy.)
2. Stir in the rice krispies, making sure they're completely covered in chocolate, and spoon into paper cake cases. Once set, keep in the fridge or at room temperature, depending on whether you like your krispie cakes crunchy, or squidgy.

cook's tip

Make a deluxe version by adding pink mini marshmallows and raisins to the mixture at Step 2 and using pastel coloured paper cake cases (Lakeland does nice ones).

Jellies

Jelly Cubes

My daughter calls these 'jubes'. They don't work nearly so well in smaller rubber moulds; the old-fashioned 1–2 inch (2.5–5cm) square hard plastic ice cube trays are best.

Maybe there's not much point in making jubes when eating them is as tricky as nailing jelly to the wall for tiny two-year-old fingers, but a big bowl of multi-coloured jelly cubes looks so good, I think it's worth it, even if most of it ends up on the floor.

2 or 3 packets of jelly, different colours

1. Make up the jellies one at a time, according to instructions on the packet, and leave to cool. One packet of jelly fills about 2½ ice cube trays, so if you've got lots, make all the jellies at once, otherwise, pop out the set jelly cubes into large food bags and re-use the trays for the next lot.
2. Pour the cold jelly into the trays and refrigerate for several hours, and preferably overnight.

cook's tip

Once the jelly is completely cold, you can put a hard jelly sweet into each cube, then leave the jelly in the fridge to set. This only works with some jelly babies, and not at all with Jelly Tots.

Cola Jelly

I usually steer clear of making anything with gelatine, partly because it seems so fiddly somehow, and partly because I'm put off by the idea that every bit of gelatine you eat stays in your body for life. But I can't help liking jelly, however undesirable its origins, and now I can't find cola-flavoured jelly in the shops, I make it at home.

If you want fizzy cola jelly, you need to add the dissolved gelatine to the cola rather than the other way around, otherwise the cola froths up too much, but I find you get a better flavour if you make the jelly with flat cola so, strange as it may seem, that's what I do.

> 4½ sheets of gelatine
> 1 pint (570ml) stale cola
> 2 teaspoons vanilla extract

1　Cut the sheets of gelatine into small pieces and put them in a bowl with 4 tablespoons cold water (4 sheets of gelatine are usually enough to set 1 pint, but it helps to have a bit extra for this recipe).
2　Leave the gelatine to break up in the cold water, then put the bowl over a small saucepan of boiling water for a few more minutes and let it dissolve completely, stirring often.
3　Pour the cola over the gelatine, add the vanilla extract, stir and put in the fridge to set for at least 6 hours and preferably overnight.

Fizzy Jelly

Fizzy jelly is no harder to make than regular still jelly and kids love it. I normally use lemonade to make a lemon or lime jelly and cherryade to make red jellies, but experiment with different combinations – there must be loads.

> 5oz (135g) block of green jelly
> ¾ pint (350ml) lemonade

1   Break the jelly into cubes and put in a very small saucepan with ¼ pint (150ml) boiling water over a very low heat, stirring occasionally until the jelly has dissolved.
2   Leave to cool *completely* – by the kitchen window is good. If you put it in the fridge, you run the risk of warming up the food inside, or you forget all about it and the jelly sets.
3   When the jelly is cold, slowly pour the lemonade into the liquid jelly, stir carefully a few times and wait a minute for any surface bubbles to settle.
4   Put in the fridge to set for at least 4 hours or overnight.

Malteser Bombe

Make a bombe instead of a birthday cake for a kid's party. Goodness knows, it's a hell of a lot quicker, easier and cheaper than trying to turn a sponge into Thomas the Tank Engine. Just before serving, pour melted chocolate over the top of the bombe and cover with a thick layer of brightly coloured hundreds and thousands, sugar flowers or crushed Smarties. Stick a lit sparkler in the centre, sing Happy Birthday very quickly before the ice cream starts melting, then remove the sparkler, give everyone a spoon and let them demolish it. These quantities are enough to fill a large Pyrex bowl (10 inches/25cm in diameter), but make it in a smaller one if you like and have leftovers. You can use other kinds of sweets in this recipe – I've used fruit-and-nut broken up into squares before – but not only is the shape of Maltesers ideal, the texture of the honeycomb in the middle stays the same when frozen, making them the best chocolates for the job. You can also make this bombe a few days, or even a couple of weeks, in advance. Keep it in the freezer and take it out when you need it.

    2 teaspoons cocoa powder or drinking chocolate
    2 teaspoons icing sugar

3½ pints (2 litres) soft scoop chocolate ice cream
2 large bags of white chocolate Maltesers
1 large bag of milk chocolate Maltesers (at least)

To decorate
cocoa powder and icing sugar, to dust
OR
2oz (50g) milk or plain chocolate, sweets or hundreds and thousands.

1   Line the Pyrex bowl with at least three layers of clingfilm with
    about an inch of surplus all around the edge. Dust the inside of
    the bowl with a mixture of cocoa powder and icing sugar to coat
    the entire surface.
2   Take the ice cream out of the freezer 10 to 15 minutes before you
    need it and have a mug of hot water on the side so you can keep
    dipping the spoon in, which makes it much, much easier to get
    the ice cream around the bowl.
3   Put two or three large spoonfuls of ice cream into the bowl at a
    time and spread a thick layer – roughly ¾ inch (2cm) – all over
    the insides of the bowl. Work quickly so the ice cream doesn't
    melt, but don't worry about making the layer of ice cream even,
    it won't be and it doesn't need to be. All you have to do is get ice
    cream around the bowl without leaving any huge gaps.
4   Pack the bombe with as many Maltesers as you can get inside
    without crushing them up.
5   Spread a final layer of ice cream over the top and cover with two
    more layers of clingfilm. Put a plate over the top, pressing down
    gently, and put the bombe in the freezer for a minimum of 4 hours.
6   Take the bombe from the freezer, turn the plate upside down and
    tip the bombe out onto the plate (because of the layers of clingfilm,
    it will easily slide out). Remove the clingfilm and dust with a
    mixture of icing sugar and cocoa powder or melt the chocolate
    and pour over the top of the bombe immediately before serving
    so the chocolate trickles down the sides (the chocolate sets hard
    in a couple of minutes).

Canapés

The word 'canapé' seems to me to imply something more complicated than what, after all, is a mere mouthful of food that only needs to look good, taste good and get from plate to person without oozing all over their fingers or, worse still, their clothes.

You can buy more elaborate canapés than these in the supermarket, frozen or otherwise, but for my money, well presented 'proper' food with lots of flavour is better than a mini Yorkshire pudding stuffed with something only vaguely recognisable, so I'd give the strawberries in a chocolate-flavoured coating a wide berth and stick with a handful of tried-and-tested recipes that only need a minimal amount of cooking, or none at all.

Chicken Satay

Thread larger pieces of chicken onto wooden skewers or cut the meat into small cubes and spear with cocktail sticks.

Makes 24 (approx)
1lb (450g) lean chicken fillets
1 tablespoon smooth peanut butter
1 tablespoon soy sauce
3½fl oz (100ml) coconut milk
1 teaspoon black treacle
1 teaspoon mustard
½ teaspoon each of ground cumin, five spice powder,
    dried coriander leaf, garlic salt and onion salt
¼ teaspoon chilli powder
lemon juice

1   Remove the skin, trim any little fatty bits off the chicken and cut the meat into roughly same-sized pieces.
2   In a medium-sized casserole dish, put the peanut butter, soy sauce, coconut milk, treacle, mustard, spices and lemon juice, according to taste. Beat everything together with a fork or a wooden spoon to make a smooth marinade.
3   Mix the meat with the marinade, then cover the dish with a lid and keep in the fridge for about 4 hours, or overnight.
4   Remove the chicken from the marinade and thread the meat onto the skewers or sticks. Grill or barbecue the chicken satay for 10 to 15 minutes, turning frequently.

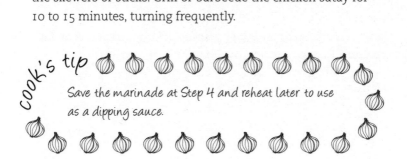

cook's tip
Save the marinade at Step 4 and reheat later to use as a dipping sauce.

Mini Crab Cakes

Serve warm or cold with a sweet chilli dipping sauce or mayonnaise mixed with a spoonful of mustard and lemon juice, according to taste.

Makes about 24
2 x tins (6oz/175g) crabmeat
2 spring onions
2 big tablespoons sesame seeds
2 teaspoons five spice powder
black pepper
lemon juice
4oz (110g) butter or margarine
3oz (75g) plain flour, plus more for dusting
½ pint (275oml) milk (approx)

1   Preheat the oven to 200c/400f/gas 6. Drain the tins of crabmeat and mix with the finely chopped spring onion and sesame seeds. Season with the five spice, black pepper and lemon juice, according to taste.

2   Melt the butter or margarine in a small saucepan, beat in the flour and cook for a minute, stirring continuously, then add the milk and whisk for a couple more minutes to make a very thick sauce.

3   Take the pan off the heat and combine the crabmeat mixture with the sauce. Shape into small cakes with your hands, using approximately one dessertspoonful of mixture at a time, and dust with flour.

4   Place the crab cakes on a well-greased baking tray and cook for 15 to 20 minutes.

Filo Pastry Parcels

Filo pastry automatically ups the glam factor of any recipe. These parcels are easy to assemble and can also be veggie-friendly, depending on what you use to fill them with. Serve warm or cold.

Makes 8–12
16 sheets (½lb/225g packet) of filo pastry
melted butter

Suggested fillings
Mushroom and pâté Poach large close cap mushrooms in stock, cool and spread smooth pâté or liver sausage in the hollow part of the mushroom.
Shredded chicken (or duck) Fry the shredded cooked meat to crisp it up and mix with hoisin sauce, barbecue sauce or mango chutney.
Veggie mix Finely chopped cooked red onion, pepper and red pesto.

1   Lightly flour a clean work surface and unroll the pastry from the packet. Preheat the oven to 200C/400F/Gas 6 or according to the instructions on the packet, and oil a couple of large baking trays.
2   Lay out three or four sheets of pastry at a time, one on top of the other, and cut into roughly 4 inch (10cm) squares.
3   Make individual parcels by arranging three or four cut squares on top of each other so the edges point out at different angles

4 Brush each layer of pastry with melted butter, put the filling in the centre of the top layer, then lift up all the layers and twist together in the middle to seal the parcel.

5 Brush with more melted butter, place on the baking trays and bake for 15 to 20 minutes, until the pastry is crisp and golden.

Crostini

Crostini is Italian for 'little crusts' or 'little toasts'. As an alternative to ready-made mini crackers, make crostini by cutting out shapes from medium-sliced brown or white bread with a small pastry cutter, then lightly toasting or baking the bread (I think you get a better result with baking).

You can also make crostini by cutting baguettes into 5mm slices or use ciabatta instead of regular sliced bread.

If you toast the bread, put it in a toast rack to cool or prop the slices up against each other in a wigwam to crisp up quickly.

To bake the bread, brush one side of each piece of cut bread with olive oil, place on an oiled baking tray and bake in a preheated 190c/375F/gas 5 oven for 5 to 10 minutes, until the bread is crisp, but has very little colour.

Top crostini with hard or soft cheeses and pickles, ham, pâté or slivers of meat – hot or cold – and small spoonfuls of sauce, such as beef and horseradish, turkey and cranberry or gammon and apple sauce. See also the Smoked Salmon Cheese on page 19.

Vol-au-vents

Still around after all these years. As an alternative to the more usual cold vol-au-vents stuffed with chicken, mushrooms or prawns, fill with chilli con carne, leftover chicken or Quorn casserole (cut everything into very small pieces) or tiny cauliflower and broccoli florets in cheese sauce and serve hot.

Quails' Eggs

Hard-boil quails' eggs by bringing them to the boil in a pan of cold water and simmering for about 2 minutes. Cool the eggs down in a bowl of cold water, tap the eggs gently on all sides and peel carefully under the water to remove the shells. Serve whole with celery salt for dipping.

Smoked Salmon Pinwheels

Use very fresh, thinly sliced brown bread (plain, not granary), cut off the crusts and don't butter. Spread a very thin layer of cream cheese on the bread and cover with strips of smoked salmon, sprinkle a little lemon juice – not too much or the bread goes soggy – season with black pepper and roll up the bread to make a cylinder. Cut into ½ inch (1cm) slices and garnish with fresh dill or parsley, and lemon slices. Alternatively, leave out the bread altogether and spread the smoked salmon with a much thicker layer of cream cheese, top with crushed walnuts, then roll up and cut into slices.

Olives on Horseback

Use the largest olives you can find, such as pimento-stuffed green olives or black olives stuffed with anchovy, jalapeño or lemon. If you have the patience, buy large pitted olives and stuff them yourself by splitting the olive down one side and filling with feta cheese, chutney or a mixture of tomato and garlic purée. Stretch rashers of streaky bacon with the back of a knife and divide each one into three strips. Wrap each olive in a strip of bacon, secure with a cocktail stick and cook under a high preheated grill for about 5 minutes, turning a couple of times, until the bacon is crisp. Serve on the cocktail sticks.

Frittata

A frittata is a thick, unfolded omelette, often cut into cubes and served cold. Any combination of ham, cheese, cooked potato, finely chopped peppers, spring onions and green beans works well, but avoid mushrooms – they discolour the omelette, which doesn't look good. Cook the omelette by melting butter in a pan and frying slices of cooked potato and finely chopped onion, pepper and green beans until golden, then add the beaten eggs and cheese to the pan and whisk the mixture a few times with a fork. Season with salt and pepper once the omelette starts to set. For best results, use a small pan so the omelette is at least an inch deep and allow to cool completely before cutting into cubes. Spear each piece with a cocktail stick to serve.

Melon in Parma Ham

This is more effective if you have a Parisienne cutter for making
the melon into balls; otherwise, cut the fruit into small, same-size
chunks. Wrap very thin strips of Parma ham around each piece of
melon to cover the fruit completely and secure with a cocktail stick.

Stuffed Dates

Medjool dates are by far the best for this, being large, very sweet
and fleshy, with an elongated pit, which makes them easy to fill once
the stones have been removed. Split the dates down one side with
a small, sharp knife and put a teaspoonful of cream cheese into the
centre. Press a whole walnut or almond into the cheese and finish
with a very light dusting of icing sugar.

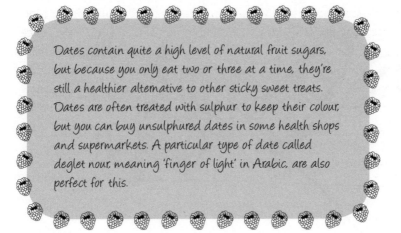

Dates contain quite a high level of natural fruit sugars,
but because you only eat two or three at a time, they're
still a healthier alternative to other sticky sweet treats.
Dates are often treated with sulphur to keep their colour,
but you can buy unsulphured dates in some health shops
and supermarkets. A particular type of date called
deglet nour, meaning 'finger of light' in Arabic, are also
perfect for this.

Girls' Night In

Personally, I prefer a girls' night out, but they're not always possible when your children are very small and/or you can't get a babysitter. If you're doing lots of food, let your friends know beforehand, otherwise you'll get everyone wailing that they've already eaten a huge dinner – and nobody likes to see chocolate cake going to waste. Obviously you don't have to restrict your girls' nights in to chocolate and cocktail recipes, but as these are two very clear favourites and we've already done kidult party food and canapés, here they are.

Chocolate and Beetroot Cake

For me, its limited appeal as a vegetable is what makes the
addition of beetroot to a chocolate cake worthwhile. It doesn't have
the melt-in-the-mouth quality of other chocolate cakes – in taste and
texture it's more like a brownie – but it's still a perfectly good cake in
its own right. The beetroot juice is used to colour the icing the same
pretty shade of pink that you'd get with cochineal, which I like, even
if chocolate cakes with pink icing are a bit on the vulgar side (which
I also like).

For the cake
1 small-medium beetroot (4oz/110g)
4oz (110g) plain chocolate
7oz (200g) self-raising flour
1oz (25g) cocoa powder
6oz (175g) margarine
6oz (175g) caster sugar
3 large eggs
splash of milk

Butter icing
3 tablespoons icing sugar
1 teaspoon cocoa powder
1 level tablespoon butter

Glacé icing
4 heaped tablespoons icing sugar
a few drops of vanilla extract

1   You can buy ready-cooked beetroot in vacuum packs, but if
    you're starting from scratch, remove the long root and stalk, cut
    the beetroot into quarters, but don't bother to peel it first; the skin
    rubs off easily once the beetroot is cooked. Put in a small saucepan
    with barely enough cold water to cover, then simmer gently for
    about half an hour until the beetroot is just soft. Save the water

the beetroot was boiled in for icing the cake later on.

2 If you buy a packet of ready-cooked beetroot, you'll have more juice than you need for the cake, so press a couple of teaspoons of concentrated juice out of the leftover beetroot (rubbing it through a sieve is one way), then save the rest for a stew.

3 Base-line two 8 inch (20cm) round cake tins with greaseproof paper and preheat the oven to 180c/350F/gas 4.

4 Break the chocolate into pieces and melt in a bowl over a pan of boiling water. Meanwhile, sift the flour and cocoa powder into a large mixing bowl, put the margarine into the bowl in small pieces and rub the fat into the dry ingredients with your fingertips until it resembles rough breadcrumbs. Make a well in the centre.

5 Put the cooked beetroot in a blender or food processor with the melted chocolate and sugar and whiz for a minute to make a paste.

6 Put the chocolate paste and the beaten eggs into the well and use a hand-held electric whisk to beat everything together, starting in the centre of the well and incorporating the ingredients a little at a time. Add a splash of milk to make a fairly soft, dropping consistency and beat for a few more seconds.

7 Divide the mixture evenly between the two cake tins, smoothing the surface with the back of the spoon, and bake in the centre of the oven for 25 to 30 minutes until the sponge is firm and springy and a skewer or sharp knife inserted into the middle of the cake comes out clean. Allow the cakes to cool completely on a wire tray.

8 Make butter icing by putting the sifted icing sugar and cocoa powder into a bowl with the butter and a few drops of hot water and beating until smooth. Sandwich both halves of the cake together.

9 Make glacé icing for the top of the cake by putting the sifted icing sugar into a bowl with the vanilla extract and a few drops of beetroot juice, then very gradually adding a little cold water, a few drops at a time, to get the right consistency. If you're using beetroot water, add a few drops at a time, stirring continuously, until you've got the icing the way you want it.

10 Pour the glacé icing over the cake, starting in the middle and using

a dinner knife dipped in hot water to spread the icing across the entire surface of the cake. Let the excess trickle down the sides of the cake and decorate the top with chocolate buttons or sugar flowers.

Flake Cake

This is the chocolate version of the Very Berry Meringue Cake on page 68, except it's a slightly bigger mixture, which works perfectly in two 9 inch (23cm) tins. The result is a larger, even more impressive cake.

6 eggs
¼ teaspoon salt
6 tablespoons milk
4oz (110g) margarine
4oz (110g) caster sugar
6oz (175g) self-raising flour
2oz (50g) cocoa powder
6oz (175g) icing sugar

To decorate
1 tablespoon hazelnuts
4 Cadbury flakes
1 small carton of double or whipping cream

1   Lightly grease and base-line two 9 inch (23cm) springform or sandwich cake tins. Preheat the oven to its lowest setting.
2   Separate the eggs. Put the whites in one mixing bowl with the salt and the egg yolks in a small bowl or measuring jug with the milk.
3   Put the margarine and caster sugar for the sponge in another mixing bowl and cream together with a hand-held electric whisk until light and fluffy, then add the egg yolks a little at a time, beating continuously.

4   Sift the flour and half the cocoa powder into the bowl and fold
    it in with a large metal spoon.
5   Divide the mixture equally between the two prepared cake tins
    as evenly as you can and quickly wash and dry the whisk blades.
6   Whisk the egg whites until stiff enough to stand up in peaks,
    then add half the icing sugar/cocoa powder at a time, whisking
    after each addition until all the sugar is incorporated and the
    meringue is as stiff as it needs to be, i.e. if you turn the bowl
    upside down, it won't fall out.
7   Spread a layer of meringue into each tin, putting slightly more
    meringue on one of the sponges and finishing with a swirl. Scatter
    the hazelnuts over the surface of the smaller sponge (that will
    be the bottom layer and the slightly larger one will be the top).
8   Bake for about 1 hour. The meringue won't colour, but the
    hazelnuts will have browned slightly by the time the cake is
    cooked. Let the cakes cool completely before taking them out of
    the tin. To do this, run a blunt knife around the edge, then release
    the spring, remove the outside of the tin carefully, turn the cakes
    over and peel away the greaseproof paper. If it's a sandwich tin,
    place a dinner plate over the top, carefully turn it over, ease the tin
    away from the cake, put another plate over the top of the cake –
    which is actually the bottom – and turn it the right way up.
9   Crumble the flakes by bashing them with a rolling pin or other
    heavy object while still in the wrapper. Whisk the cream until
    thick, then spread over the nutty half of the cake and cover with
    half the chocolate. Put the other cake on top and sprinkle the
    rest of the chocolate over the surface.
10 Keep in the fridge and eat within three days.

Maddie's Brownies

This recipe was passed on to me by my daughter's friend, Maddie
Richardson, who's famous at school for her amazing melting

brownies, which she says should be 'molten inside with a light crispy layer on top'. The secret is to undercook the brownies by 10 to 15 minutes, so they're soft and fudgy in the centre, but if you'd rather your brownies had a more regular cake-like texture, keep them in the oven for the full 30 to 35 minutes.

Makes 16 squares
8oz (225g) unsalted butter
2 × 4oz (110g) plain chocolate bars
7oz (200g) self-raising flour
1oz (25g) cocoa powder
3 eggs
8oz (225g) caster sugar

1 Preheat the oven to 180C/350F/gas 4. Lightly grease and long-strip-line a rectangular 30 × 20 × 4cm (12 × 8 × 1½ inch) baking tin with greaseproof paper or baking parchment.
2 Start melting the butter in a bowl over a pan of boiling water. When it's almost done, add the chocolate in small pieces, stirring occasionally until butter and chocolate have melted completely.
3 Meanwhile, sift the flour and cocoa powder together.
4 In a large mixing bowl, beat the eggs and sugar together with a hand-held electric whisk on high speed until pale and fluffy, then turn down to the lowest setting, pour in the chocolate mixture and whisk continuously for another minute.
5 Add the sifted flour and cocoa powder, a couple of tablespoons at a time, and either fold it in with a large metal spoon or, for speed, carry on using the whisk on the slowest setting.
6 Pour the mixture into the prepared tin and bake for 20 to 25 minutes until the top is just set. Leave to cool completely in the tin – at least a couple of hours – then lift the cake out of the tin, cut into squares and refrigerate.

White Chocolate Cherry Brownies

These are delish and if you reduce the cooking time by about
10 minutes, as per Maddie's brownies (see page 196), they're even
better. Cut into tiny squares and keep in the fridge. One small piece
at a time is all you need and they're good for at least a week.

Makes 16 squares
8ozz (225g) unsalted butter
8oz (225g) white chocolate
3 eggs
8oz (225g) caster sugar
8oz (225g) self-raising flour
½ small jar of maraschino cherries (approx)
2 teaspoons vanilla extract

1 Preheat the oven to 180c/350F/gas 4. Lightly grease and long-
   strip-line a rectangular 30 × 20 × 4cm (12 × 8 × 1½ inch) baking
   tin with greaseproof paper or baking parchment.
2 Start melting the butter in a bowl over a pan of boiling water.
   When it's almost done, add the chocolate in small pieces, stirring
   occasionally until butter and chocolate have melted completely.
3 In a large mixing bowl, beat the eggs and sugar together with a
   hand-held electric whisk on high speed until pale and fluffy, then
   turn down to the lowest setting and pour in the chocolate mixture,
   whisking continuously for another minute.
4 Fold in the sifted flour with a large metal spoon or, for speed, carry
   on using the whisk on the slowest setting.
5 Add the cherries – whole or cut into smaller pieces, it's up to you –
   and vanilla extract and stir well to distribute the fruit evenly.
6 Pour the mixture into the prepared tin and bake for 30 to 35
   minutes until the top is just set. Leave to cool completely in the
   tin – at least a couple of hours – then lift the cake out of the tin,
   cut into squares and refrigerate.

Mud Pie

When I run out of milk chocolate, which often happens, I make this mud pie with plain, and when I'm out of chocolate altogether, I make it with cocoa powder instead. (In which case, sift 2 tablespoons of cocoa powder into the whisked sugar and egg mixture before the butter and syrup at Step 4, folding it in with a large metal spoon.)

Expect the surface to split and crack a little during the cooking time, and be sure to leave the cake in the tin to cool down completely before you take it out. Even when they're cold, mud pies always sink a little in the middle when you get them out of the tin; try and move them when they're still warm and they cave in completely like a Roman ruin. That said, mud pies are unfailingly delicious, whatever they look like.

12 chocolate digestive biscuits
2oz (50g) butter
4oz (110g) butter or margarine
2 tablespoons golden syrup
4oz (110g) milk chocolate
a few drops of vanilla extract
1 teaspoon instant coffee dissolved in 1 tablespoon boiling water
2 teaspoons cocoa powder
3 large eggs
8oz (225g) caster sugar

To serve
icing sugar and cocoa powder, to dust
ice cream or sour berries and single cream

1   Crumble the biscuits in a bowl with your fingers or put them between two layers of greaseproof paper and crush them up with a rolling pin. Melt the butter in a small saucepan, add the biscuit crumbs and mix well. Lightly grease and base-line an 8 inch (20cm) round cake tin, then press the mixture into the tin in an even layer.
2   Preheat the oven to 180C/350F/gas 4.

3 Melt the butter or margarine and golden syrup together (in the same small saucepan you used to make the base). At the same time, melt the chocolate in a bowl over a pan of hot water, adding the vanilla extract and coffee. When the chocolate has completely melted, stir in the sifted cocoa powder.

4 In a large mixing bowl, beat the eggs and sugar with a hand-held electric whisk on high speed until pale and fluffy, then turn the whisk down to its lowest setting and pour in the melted butter and syrup followed by the chocolate mixture, whisking continuously for a minute until everything is combined.

5 Pour the mixture onto the biscuit base and bake in the lower half of the oven for 1 hour to 1 hour and 15 minutes, until a skewer or sharp knife inserted into the middle comes out clean.

6 Leave to cool down completely, then take the mud pie out of the tin and refrigerate.

7 When cold, dust the mud pie with icing sugar or a mixture of cocoa powder and icing sugar and serve with ice cream or sour berries and single cream.

Cosmopolitan

This has been around since the 1980s, but was made famous in recent years by *Sex and the City*. Perfect for making well in advance and keeping in the fridge for later.

Serves 6
2 oranges
3 limes
raspberries
strawberries
½ pint (275ml) vodka
1 shot glass of Cointreau
¼ pint (150ml) cranberry juice
a big splash of lime juice

1 Wash the oranges and limes, cut into sixths or eighths, then halve each segment and make sure all the pips are removed. Wash and dry a large handful each of raspberries and strawberries. Halve the strawberries and leave the raspberries whole.
2 Put all the fruit in a large cut glass bowl, pour on the alcohol, cranberry juice and lime and stir gently.
3 Cover in clingfilm and keep in the fridge. Serve in chilled martini glasses.

Mojito

Another classic, there are lots of theories regarding the origin of the name, which could be a derivative of *mojadito*, Spanish for 'a little wet' or relate to the word *mojo*, a Cuban seasoning made from lime. Also nice – but not at all classic – made with a splash of lime cordial and half this amount of sugar syrup.

Serves 6
ice cubes
½ pint (275ml) Bacardi
¼ pint (150ml) soda water
7fl oz (200ml) sugar syrup (see page 233)
lime juice
3 limes
fresh mint

1 Half-fill a pitcher with ice cubes, then pour on the Bacardi, soda water, sugar syrup and lime juice, according to taste.
2 Add the limes, cut into quarters, and a big handful of fresh mint (remove the thicker stalks, but don't tear or cut the leaves).
3 Stir two or three times and top up the pitcher with more ice cubes.
4 Serve in short glasses or highball glasses with a fresh sprig of mint and a black straw.

Country Girl

This is made with the Apple Brandy on page 229, but if you don't have apple brandy, mix approximately 1 part brandy with 3 parts clear apple juice. Serve in tall 'highball' glasses

Serves 6
crushed ice
½ pint (275ml) Apple Brandy liqueur
1 pint (570ml) pink lemonade
2 small bright red apples
maraschino cherries

1   Fill six highball glasses with crushed ice about one third of the way up, then put a measure of apple brandy in each one.
2   Top up with pink lemonade and garnish with thinly cut apple slices and cherries.

Rosy Cheek

Serves 6
½ watermelon
½ pint (275ml) strawberry vodka
2 teaspoons vanilla extract
1–2 tablespoons runny honey
crushed ice

Garnish
watermelon segments
strawberries

1   Crush the watermelon to a rough pulp by pulsing in a food processor or putting into a large container with a tight-fitting lid and shaking hard for a minute or two.

2   Fine strain the watermelon through a sieve lined with a thin
    cotton cloth.
3   Put all ingredients together and shake well to blend everything
    together, then pour the cocktail into a pitcher and top up with
    crushed ice.
4   Garnish with whole fresh strawberries or slices of watermelon
    cut into fan-shaped segments. Serve in chilled martini glasses.

Desperate Housewife

The Desperate Housewife is a combination of gin and orange, just
like grandma used to make, with cleansing cranberry juice, sugar
syrup for sweetening, very crushed ice and an optimistic sprig of
mint. What else could you possibly call it?

Serves 6
crushed ice
½ pint (275ml) gin
7fl oz (200ml) smooth orange juice
4fl oz (120ml) cranberry juice
2fl oz (55ml) sugar syrup (see page 233)

Garnish
1 large orange for paring and slicing into rings
sprigs of fresh mint

1   Top and tail the orange by cutting a thick slice from each end so
    the orange rests flat on the chopping board and you can clearly
    see the fruit inside.
2   Use a very sharp small knife to pare thin slices of peel,
    approximately ½ inch (1cm) wide, from the top to the bottom
    of the orange. Gently scrape the pith away from the peel (that
    way you get the flavour and aroma of the orange without any
    of the bitterness).

3 Trim any remaining pith from the whole orange and cut the fruit
   into thick rings.
4 Fill a third of a pitcher with crushed ice; pour in the gin,
   orange juice, cranberry juice and sugar syrup. Stir. Add the orange
   parings and rings and top the pitcher up with more crushed ice
   if necessary.
5 Serve in cold highball glasses or goblets, including pieces of the
   fruit and peel, and garnish each cocktail with a fresh sprig of mint.

Elderflower Power

Serves 6
½ pint (275ml) gin
½ pint (275ml) cloudy apple juice
4fl oz (120ml) elderflower cordial (see page 240)
1–2 tablespoons syrup from a jar of maraschino cherries
ice cubes

Garnish
elderflowers
maraschino cherries
cocktail sticks

1 Put all liquid ingredients into a pitcher, stir well and fill the pitcher
   to the brim with hard ice cubes.
2 Serve in cold highball glasses and garnish each cocktail with fresh
   elderflowers and maraschino cherries on cocktail sticks.

Passion Fruit Killer

A non-alcoholic cocktail, because there has to be one.

Serves 6
4–6 ripe passion fruit
1 pint (570ml) cloudy apple juice
½ pint (275ml) lemonade (approx)
1 tablespoon runny honey
crushed ice

1   Scoop out the flesh and seeds of the passion fruit and put in a pitcher with the rest of the ingredients.
2   Half-fill six tall glasses with crushed ice, top up with the cocktail, stir and serve with straws.

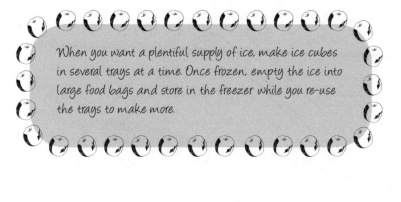

When you want a plentiful supply of ice, make ice cubes in several trays at a time. Once frozen, empty the ice into large food bags and store in the freezer while you re-use the trays to make more.

One for the Boys

I don't mean to imply that men can't fend for themselves occasionally or that it's necessarily a girl's job to cook for the boys before a night out, but these easy one-pot dinners are very man-friendly. Make one yourself in less time than it takes to put your make-up on, or tell the man in your life how it's done and leave him to get on with it.

Mexican Chicken Wraps

Swap the jalapeños for hotter chillies if you like, and double up on the spices for larger amounts of chicken. As a rough guide, one chicken fillet makes two wraps.

Serves 4
4 large chicken fillets
2 peppers, red or green
3–4 jalapeños
1 red onion
oil
4 teaspoons ground cumin
4 teaspoons ground coriander
1 teaspoon garlic salt
1 teaspoon hot chilli powder
1 small iceberg lettuce
tomatoes
cucumber
1 packet of flour or corn tortillas

1   Remove the chicken skin, wash and trim off any little fatty bits, then cut the chicken into thin strips.
2   Thinly slice the peppers and jalapeños (remove the seeds to reduce the heat) and finely chop the red onion.
3   Warm some oil in a very large frying pan while you mix the spices together on a dinner plate. Coat the meat in the spices and quickly brown the chicken strips in the hot oil.
4   Turn the heat down, add the pepper, jalapeño and onion and fry for about 10 minutes until the meat is cooked through and the onion is soft.
5   Meanwhile, shred the iceberg lettuce and slice the tomatoes and cucumber.
6   Warm the tortillas according to the packet instructions, then wrap around the hot chicken and salad and serve.

Chips and Curry Sauce

Makes at least 6 large helpings
oil
1 onion
3 carrots
3 apples
1 big tablespoon curry powder
2 teaspoons ground cumin
2 teaspoons ground cinnamon
2 teaspoons allspice
2 tablespoons plain flour
1 tablespoon instant gravy granules
½ tube tomato purée
1 teaspoon sugar
1 teaspoon salt
oven chips

1   Warm some oil in a very large pan over a low heat while you peel
    and roughly chop up the onion, carrots and apples.
2   Mix the curry powder, cumin, cinnamon and allspice together and
    add the spices to the hot oil, followed by the fruit and vegetables.
3   Cook over a low heat for a few minutes until the onion has
    softened a bit, then sift in the flour and cook for another minute.
4   Pour 1 pint (570ml) boiling water into the pan, stir well, then add
    the instant gravy granules and stir again.
5   Add the tomato purée, sugar and salt, then cover the pan with
    a lid and leave the sauce to simmer gently for 20 to 30 minutes.
6   Meanwhile, preheat the oven to 200c/400f/gas 6 and spread out
    as many oven chips as you need on a large baking tray (or two).
    Drizzle the chips with oil and cook the chips in the usual way.
7   Once the carrots in the curry sauce are cooked through, blend
    the finished sauce in a food processor and serve with the chips.
    The curry sauce keeps in the fridge for about a week.

Chinese Meatballs

Serves 4
1 red or green pepper
1 onion
½lb (225g) mushrooms
2 teaspoons ground ginger
black pepper
1–1½ pints (570–850ml) beef stock
2 cloves of garlic
1 teaspoon salt
2 teaspoons five spice powder
1lb (450g) lean steak mince
1 large glass of sherry
3–4 tablespoons tomato purée
soy sauce
dried noodles (3–4 large squares)

1   Finely chop the pepper, onion and mushrooms and put the vegetables in a very large saucepan with 1 teaspoon of the ginger and some black pepper.
2   Make 1 pint of beef stock with 1 stock cube and pour enough of the liquid into the saucepan to just cover the vegetables. Cook over a low heat for about 10 minutes until the onion has softened.
3   Meanwhile, mix the crushed garlic with the salt, the rest of the ginger and all the five spice powder. Put the paste into a bowl with the mince and squish it all together with your hands before making into small meatballs, roughly the size of a large marble – you should get about 30 meatballs from this amount of meat.
4   Turn the heat up under the pan and pour in the rest of the beef stock with the sherry, tomato purée and a couple of big splashes of soy sauce.
5   As soon as the stock is boiling, add the meatballs to the pan, turn the heat down a little and simmer for 10 to 15 minutes until the meatballs are cooked through. Make a little more stock with

another stock cube to add to the pan at this stage if you think you
need more liquid.

6   Break up the noodles a bit, put them in the pan and stir well.
Simmer for a few more minutes, stirring occasionally until the
noodles are just soft, then serve.

One Pot Stew

This is perfect with the remains of a curry, casserole or goulash,
or any leftover meat.

Serves 2–4
Leftover cooked meat (approx 1lb [500g]) or the remains of a casserole
1 tin of potatoes
1 tin of carrots
1 tin of butter beans
1 tin of garden peas
1 tin of Eazy fried onions
1 stock cube
Any seasoning you like

1   Open all the tins. (Size doesn't matter, and if you're making this
for more than four people you'll probably need to double up on
some of them.)
2   Empty all the tins into a very large saucepan discarding some
of the liquid if putting it all in would make the stew too watery,
as it will if your leftover meat dish already includes lots of gravy.
3   Warm up the stew over a gentle heat; crumble in the stock cube,
add seasoning and stir occasionally until everything is piping hot.
Serve with crusty bread.

Hangover Cures

The surest way to avoid a hangover is not to drink too much in the first place, obviously. Failing that, prevention is better than cure, but when that dreadful morning after feeling can't be prevented or cured, you'll have to rely on damage limitation to help make it better.

I ought to point out that the following suggestions *are* just suggestions, not foolproof solutions, but beware of the hair of the dog theory. All that does is keep the main hangover at bay a little longer.

The Night Before

- Eat carbs and starchy foods for dinner: pasta in a tomato-based sauce, jacket potatoes, baked beans on toast, The Ultimate Fish Finger Sandwich (see page 93) or Hot Beef Goulash and rice (see page 105).
- If you can't eat a proper meal beforehand, at least have a glass of milk and a couple of plain biscuits, e.g. gingernuts, rich teas or digestives.
- Alternate every alcoholic drink with a soft drink, or preferably water.
- Try not to mix your drinks, but if you can't help having beer and wine on the same night, have them in that order. As the saying goes, 'Beer before wine makes you feel fine, wine before beer makes you feel queer,' (or something like that). The other thing you're not meant to do is mix grape and grain, so no whisky chasers after the wine.
- Stick to white wine and light spirits. Red wine, whisky, dark rum

and other coloured drinks contain more chemicals, making them more likely to give you a headache.

- A bag of chips on the way home – big fat ones from a proper fish and chip shop – does the trick for some people.
- Drink two glasses of water before you go to bed and try and sip the second one over a period of at least a few minutes so it hydrates, rather than going straight through you.
- Pop a couple of soluble painkillers in a glass of water at bedtime, e.g. Solpadeine Plus. Apparently, soluble tablets get to the source of the pain more quickly than other kinds.

The Morning After

- Alka Seltzer Plus or Andrews Liver Salts settle your stomach, have a cleansing effect and detoxify the liver.
- Dehydration is a major consequence of too much alcohol and an isotonic drink containing salts in the same concentration as the ones in your body helps to restore the balance. Make your own isotonic drink with ½ pint (275ml) water, 1 teaspoon sugar, a pinch of salt and a big splash of lemon and/or lime juice.
- Feverfew is a herbal remedy for headaches or take soluble painkillers (as per The Night Before).
- Fresh rosehips are good for hangovers apparently, but because most of us don't have fresh rosehips around when we need them, try making an alternative version with rosehip syrup. Mix 1 part syrup with 5 parts hot, previously boiled water and add a pinch of salt, ½ teaspoon bicarbonate of soda and some grated (or ground) ginger. In fact, ready-made rosehip syrup isn't always easy to find either, but Lakeland stocks lovely rosehip syrup made by Atkins and Potts, or order it online, in anticipation.
- Eat something as soon as you get up – assuming you can keep food down – e.g. porridge made with milk, tomato juice with a splash of Worcestershire sauce, fresh carrot, celery and apple juice or the

high-energy banana and yoghurt breakfast on page 141.

- Eat more. A fry-up is a classic hangover cure, but it shouldn't be too heavy or overloaded with grease, so have either bacon or sausages, not both, preferably grilled or oven-baked, and scrambled or poached eggs instead of fried.
- Eggs are a good bet generally because they contain the amino acid cysteine, an effective antioxidant, so eat them any way you like.
- Other tried-and-tested recipes include Kedgeree (the cheat's version is on page 84), sausages and mash with lashings of mustard and the Chips and Curry Sauce (see page 208).
- Keep sipping water at regular intervals throughout the day or drink pomegranate juice, a powerful antioxidant, which improves blood flow and boosts energy levels.
- Have a shower and alternate between hot and cold water, concentrating the stream of water at the base of the skull.
- Someone I know swears she once kept a hangover at bay all day just by lying down for long periods of time with a warm lavender bag at the back of her neck. (Reheat the bag in the microwave every half hour or so.)
- A fizzy drink such as lemonade or just plain tonic water can help to clear the last of the headache once you're on the mend.
- Get some fresh air – and try and remember how bad you feel for the next time.

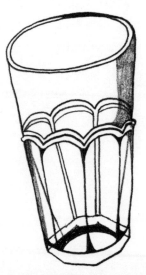

Sugar and Spice

'1. All things nice, especially in relation to fruit, confectionery and certain alcoholic beverages.'

This chapter needs no explanation really, other than to say it's nice to experiment with food and drink for the pure, simple enjoyment of tasting something you've made and because, not only is there very little cooking involved in most of these recipes, the results should be around for at least a few days, if not weeks. When your regular eating and cheating routine is a never-ending cycle of breakfast, lunch, dinner, snacks and packed lunches, you forget there's more to cooking than making a meal that disappears in a matter of minutes, leaving you wondering where the next one's coming from and who's going to help with the washing up. These good old-fashioned recipes for sweets, drinks and preserves will help you get in touch with your inner Mrs Beeton and provide a little light relief from all that.

Sweets

We're used to the idea that sweets and sugary drinks are,
at best, superfluous to our daily requirements and, at worst,
a completely unnecessary evil. So it's quite shocking to find
recommendations for candies and cordials made from cream
and sugar as a form of nourishment in very old books, until
you remember that when these recipes were written – well
over a hundred years ago in most cases – people lived on a
pure whole food diet, which included relatively tiny amounts
of sugar and no processed foods *at all*. It's also easy to forget
that everyone, especially children, needs a certain amount of
fat in their diet, even now, and in the days when people lived
in much colder, harsher conditions than we do, they needed
all the calories they could get. Imagine that.

Fudge

There are various ways of making fudge. This is my favourite because the result is not too sticky, not too soft and it works like a charm every time.

The quantities given here make 36 squares in an 8 inch (20cm) cake tin, but you can easily make less by halving all the ingredients, in which case you shouldn't need to boil the mixture for any longer than 15 minutes (start testing after 10 minutes).

Stand the pan in a bowl of cold water to cool it down quickly at the beating stage. After a couple of minutes the fudge starts to thicken and lose its shine, becoming dull and slightly grainy, then all you have to do is add any flavouring you want – vanilla extract, coffee essence or melted chocolate – and get it into the tin.

Makes 36 squares
6oz (175g) unsalted butter
1 tin of evaporated milk
roughly ¼ pint (150ml) milk
2lb (900g) sugar

Flavourings
1 teaspoon instant coffee dissolved in 1 tablespoon boiling water
2 teaspoons vanilla extract
3oz (75g) plain chocolate

1 Melt the butter in a large saucepan while you lightly grease and long-strip-line an 8 inch (20cm) square cake tin.
2 Pour the tin of evaporated milk into a measuring jug, then top up to the 1 pint (570ml) mark with the milk. Add the milk and sugar to the saucepan, stir well and leave over a low heat for about 5 minutes, stirring occasionally, until the sugar has dissolved.
3 Bring to the boil, then boil rapidly for 15 to 20 minutes, stirring continuously, until a drop of the syrup dropped into a cup of cold water holds its shape when squeezed (i.e. the soft ball stage).

4   Remove the pan from the heat and beat constantly as the fudge cools down, then add your chosen flavouring and scrape it into the prepared tin.

5   Mark the fudge into squares after about 15 minutes; leave it in the tin for at least two hours to cool completely, then lift it out, cut it up and store in an airtight tin.

Chocolate Nut Crunches

These quantities are exactly right for making 18 perfect, same-size sweeties, but you may want to start with more chocolate than this so you've got plenty to play with at the dipping stage. (That way you can allow for a certain amount of waste...)

Makes 18
8oz (225g) milk chocolate
6–8 Blue Riband chocolate wafers
1–2 tablespoons single cream
1 egg yolk
2oz (50g) butter
2oz (50g) whole hazelnuts
4oz (110g) crushed hazelnuts

1   Break three-quarters of the milk chocolate bar (6oz/150g) into small pieces, put the pieces into a heatproof bowl and leave to melt over a pan of boiling water, stirring occasionally.

2   Meanwhile, bash each one of the chocolate wafers once with a rolling pin, or something similar, while they're still in the wrappers.

3   Once the chocolate has melted completely, add the cream, egg yolk and butter in that order, quickly mix everything together with a metal tablespoon, then take the bowl off the heat, open the wrappers and tip the wafers straight into the bowl.

4   Stir the mixture a few times – just enough to combine everything without breaking the wafers up too much and reducing them to

mush – then put the bowl in the fridge and leave the mixture to set into a workable paste for about half an hour.

5   Melt the remaining 2oz (50g) of chocolate in another bowl (this is enough to coat 18 sweets, but use more chocolate if you're not sure). Put the whole hazelnuts on a small plate and spread the crushed hazelnuts out on a large plate.

6   Press a teaspoonful of the chocolate mixture around a whole hazelnut, then form the mixture into a ball with the palms of your hands. Dip each ball in the melted chocolate to coat as thinly as possible, then roll the sweets in the crushed hazelnuts. Leave to set at room temperature for about an hour. Store in an airtight tin or wrap individually in foil or cellophane.

Coconut Ice

Most coconut ice recipes leave out the spoonful of butter and you don't really need it, but it does give the sweets a slightly softer texture, which I like, so put it in or leave it out, it's up to you.

Makes 12–16 squares
1lb (450g) caster sugar
4oz (110g) desiccated coconut
2 teaspoons butter
few drops of pink food colouring

1   Lightly butter a non-stick 6 inch (15cm) cake tin, round or square.

2   Put the sugar and ¼ pint (150ml) water in a large saucepan over a low heat. As soon as the sugar dissolves, turn the heat up a bit and boil fairly rapidly until a drop of the syrup dropped into a cup of cold water can be squeezed into a soft ball. This should take between 5 and 10 minutes.

3   Take the pan off the heat and stir in the coconut immediately, followed by the butter.

4   Working quickly – the mixture sets hard very quickly – press half into the tin and colour the rest of the mixture with a few drops of pink food colouring. Cover the white half with a layer of pink coconut ice and mark into squares.

5   Leave for at least 1 hour to cool and set completely, then cut the coconut ice into squares and store in an airtight tin for up to three weeks.

Orange Creams

To break up the sugary texture of the finished sweets, add hazelnuts, pistachios, chopped stem ginger, dried figs or desiccated coconut – or a combination of all of these.

Makes approx 24 squares
2lb (900g) granulated sugar
14fl oz (400ml) single cream
finely grated zest of 1 orange
few drops of orange extract

1   Put the sugar and cream in a large saucepan and bring slowly to the boil, stirring frequently. Meanwhile, lightly grease a 6 to 8 inch (15–20cm) square tin with butter or margarine.

2   Boil gently for a few minutes and when the syrup is noticeably thicker, drop ½ teaspoon of the cream into a cup of cold water; if you can squeeze it into a soft ball, it's ready.

3   Take the pan off the heat and stir in the orange zest and a few drops of orange extract, or whatever flavouring you're using.

4   Lower the pan carefully into a bowl of cold water; when the water splutters out of control, lift the pan out of the bowl and lower it in again. This time it should just hiss a bit.

5   With the pan standing in the bowl of water, beat the cream with a wooden spoon and as soon as it starts to look slightly grainy –

this won't take a minute – quickly pour the mixture into the
prepared tin and smooth it down with the back of a metal spoon.

6   Mark into small squares and leave for at least an hour or two to
     cool and set completely before cutting up. Keep the creams in a
     plastic box or a tin and eat within two weeks.

Fruit Leather

This idea was passed on to me by a friend who lives in the depths
of the countryside and who's very keen on experimental recipes
with fruit and vegetables, especially the ones she's foraged
for herself.

Anyway, I made my fruit leather with blueberries (foraged from
the supermarket) and even though there are plenty of other ways
to eat berries, I always think it's worth putting a wacky recipe to the
test – as long as it's a dead easy one – because it's fascinating to see
how it works.

Instead of drying the fruit out in the oven, you can put the tray
in the airing cupboard and forget about it for a while (not to the
extent of dumping a pile of towels on top of it though), then let
it stand at room temperature for a couple of hours before cutting
the fruit leather into strips.

> 2 tablespoons sugar
> 1lb (450g) blueberries

1   Put the sugar and 4fl oz (125ml) water in a small saucepan
     and heat very gently for 20 to 30 minutes until all the sugar has
     dissolved, then bring to the boil and simmer fairly rapidly to reduce
     the amount of syrup by about half.

2   Meanwhile, completely line a baking tray with greaseproof paper
     or cover the tray with clingfilm and place a sheet of greaseproof
     paper on top. Don't grease or oil the paper.

3   Purée the fruit in a blender or food processor and stir in the cooled
    syrup, then press the mixture evenly over the paper to a depth of
    about 3mm.
4   Put in the oven at the lowest setting – leave the door open slightly
    if you're worried your oven is too hot – and leave for an absolute
    minimum of 6 hours, then leave to rest at room temperature
    for a few more hours until the fruit is completely cool and dry.
    When the leather's ready, it will peel cleanly away from the paper.
5   Cut the fruit leather into strips and put back onto the greaseproof
    paper, which can then be rolled up loosely and kept in a sealed
    container in the fridge for two or three days.

Peppermint Creams dipped in Chocolate

You'll never find an easier sweet to make than this one. For mint-
green creams, add a very few drops of green food colouring
to the icing sugar with the peppermint oil.

> **Makes 32 (approx)**
> 1 egg white
> 1lb (450g) icing sugar
> few drops of peppermint oil (or peppermint essence, but oil is better)
> 4oz (110g) plain chocolate bar

1   Beat the egg white with a hand-held electric whisk until fluffy
    but not stiff, then stir in the sifted icing sugar with a few drops of
    peppermint oil, and food colouring if you're making green sweets.
2   Squeeze the mixture together with your hand to make a smooth
    paste, then break off small pieces at a time and roll into balls,
    roughly the size of marbles.
3   flatten the balls into discs and press each one with a fork on one
    side to make lines. Leave the sweets on a sheet of greaseproof
    paper to dry for about 2 hours.

4   Melt the chocolate in a bowl over a pan of boiling water. Stick a small, sharp knife into the unmarked side of the sweets and dip into the melted chocolate one at a time. Leave the sweets to dry out for another couple of hours and store in an airtight tin for up to four months.

Honeycomb

8 heaped tablespoons sugar
8 heaped tablespoons golden syrup
4 rounded teaspoons bicarbonate of soda

1   Lightly oil a sheet of greaseproof paper and put it in a shallow bowl, plate or cake tin.
2   Put the sugar, golden syrup and 4 tablespoons water in a large saucepan over a moderate heat, mix it all together and stir continuously with a wooden spoon.
3   Let the syrup boil for up to 5 minutes – keep your eye on the clock – by which time it should be a rich, golden brown (but not too dark, you don't want it burnt).
4   Quickly add the bicarbonate of soda, still stirring rapidly, and get the pan off the heat as the honeycomb froths and rises up the pan.
5   Scrape the honeycomb onto the greaseproof paper immediately and leave to set for about an hour before breaking it up into chunks.

Peanut Brittle

Plain, unsalted peanuts are much cheaper from Asian shops or the specialist food aisle in the supermarket, so try and avoid those pretty little packets of nuts and seeds in the organic and health food sections. They look nice, but cost considerably more.

Once the peanuts have been soaked in very hot water for a couple of minutes, the red skins slide off easily. The annoying bit is having to separate the nuts from the soggy skins in the bowl, so be prepared to spend 15 minutes on what ought to be a 2 minute job – or cheat by getting the kids to do it for you.

That said, peanut brittle is one of those things you don't come across very often these days, even though lots of people still love it, so it's definitely worth making.

Makes about 10 rounds of brittle
½lb (225g) unsalted nuts
1lb (450g) Demerera sugar
few drops of almond essence

1   Preheat the oven to 170c/325F/gas 3. Soak the peanuts in very hot water for a few minutes, then strain through a colander and transfer the nuts to a bowl of cold water. Separate from the skins (see above).
2   Spread the nuts out on a large ovenproof tray and put them in the oven for about 15 minutes until they're completely dry and a light golden brown in colour.
3   Meanwhile, put the sugar and ¼ pint (150ml) water in a large saucepan and bring to the boil. Add the nuts to the pan and boil quite rapidly, stirring frequently, until the syrup is golden brown and ½ teaspoon dropped into a cup of cold water makes a fairly brittle strand.
4   Take the pan off the heat and add the almond essence. Use a dessertspoon to drop circles of the mixture onto a lightly oiled sheet of greaseproof paper and work quickly as the syrup sets

hard in less than 2 minutes. Leave for about a quarter of an hour, then lift the circles of peanut brittle off the paper and store in a plastic box or a tin for up to two weeks.

Petits Fours

I think of petits fours as sweets, but they're really tiny cakes. The name means 'small oven' because in the eighteenth century petits fours were put into brick ovens after much larger cakes had been baked and the ovens were cooling down. Petit four cases can be found beside the other cake cases in the supermarket – the gold and silver ones are perfect for these – otherwise you can pipe the paste straight onto a lightly greased oven tray. Make a chocolate version by swapping 1oz (25g) flour for 1oz (25g) cocoa powder.

Makes at least 24
4oz (110g) butter
1 egg
4oz (110g) plain flour
1oz (25g) ground almonds
1oz (25g) caster sugar

To decorate
glacé cherries
angelica
pistachios
hazelnuts
miniature sweet jellies
sugar flowers

1   Lightly grease two ovenproof trays and preheat the oven to 180C/350F/gas 4.
2   In a large bowl, cream the butter and sugar until pale and fluffy, then beat in the egg, whisking all the time.

3   Fold in the sifted flour and ground almonds to make a stiff mixture halfway between a cake batter and a paste.
4   Use a star-shaped nozzle to pipe the mixture onto the trays, making tiny biscuits roughly the size of a two pence piece, then decorate with a sweet or a piece of candied fruit. Bake for 10 minutes until crisp and only just golden. Cool on a wire tray and store in an airtight tin for up to two weeks.

Toffee

To make a fruit-flavoured toffee, leave out the vinegar and stir in two tablespoons seedless jelly or jam at Step 3.

> 4oz (110g) butter
> ½lb (225g) granulated or soft brown sugar
> 2 tablespoons golden syrup
> 2 tablespoons vinegar

1   Lightly grease a shallow 6 inch (15cm) cake tin, while you melt the butter in a large saucepan over a low heat.
2   Add the rest of the ingredients and boil gently until all the sugar has dissolved, then turn the heat up and boil fairly rapidly, stirring occasionally, until the mixture is golden brown and a little of the syrup dropped into a cup of cold water is hard and brittle.
3   Scrape the mixture into the tin and leave to cool for half an hour. Mark the toffee into squares and leave for another couple of hours until the toffee is completely cold and set. Break into squares and store in a plastic box or a tin for a few weeks.

Drinks

Both the recipes for alcoholic and non-alcoholic drinks are very straightforward and require only the most basic equipment. Everything that needs to be sterilised can be treated in one of the following ways:

- Put through the dishwasher
- Immersed in boiling water for 10 minutes
- Soaked in Milton fluid according to the directions on the packaging

There's loads of room for manoeuvre with the quantities in most of these recipes, just remember an average size mug = roughly ½ pint (275ml) of liquid or ½lb (225g) sugar, which is as much accuracy as you need, so you don't even have to use a set of scales and a measuring jug if you don't want to.

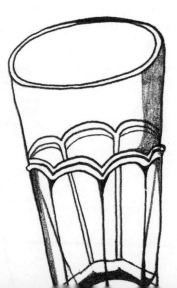

Liqueurs and alcoholic drinks

I would never have thought of making my own liqueurs until I met
Patricia Stockham, a very enthusiastic cook with a massive collection
of books, who I got to know after she wrote to tell me off for putting
too many carrots in a carrot cake recipe, and to whom I'm eternally
grateful for giving me the idea and telling me how it's done. Now I'm
hooked, and can honestly say an afternoon spent making liqueurs
is very nearly as much fun as an evening spent drinking them.
Homemade liqueurs also make great presents, especially at
Christmas, and if you make enough, you'll have a base for a cocktail
and something to pour into and over any number of desserts and
puddings all year round.

The basic ingredients are sugar syrup, fruit and alcohol and there
are no real rules about quantities. If a liqueur turns out too thick
and syrupy, all you need to do is dilute it with more alcohol. And if
you're usually wary of buying supermarket own-brand alcohol, don't
be. The cheaper varieties are perfect for making liqueurs, so stock
up on the gin, vodka, whisky and brandy. I've used them all and they
do the job just fine.

A large glass jar with a capacity of roughly 1½–2 pints (850ml–
1.25 litres) and a tight-fitting lid is ideal for the first stage, and if you
have enough of these, you can make several different liqueurs –
or vast quantities of one or two favourites – in the same afternoon.
Once the liqueurs are ready to drink a couple of months down the
line, they only need to be strained and decanted into small wine
bottles. That's it.

Apple Brandy

Use a mixture of apples – including windfalls if you've got apple trees nearby – and leave the cores and pips in. You could also use pears, or a mixture of apples and pears, or quinces, which should be simmered for an extra 20 minutes once the syrup has reached boiling point.

½lb (225g) caster or soft brown sugar
½ pint (275ml) water
2lb (900g) apples
5–6 cloves
½ bottle of brandy

1   Put the sugar and water in a saucepan and heat very slowly until all the sugar has dissolved.
2   Meanwhile, give the apples a good wash with a nailbrush, then cut into quarters or eighths, depending on the size of the apples.
3   Put the apples and cloves in the warm syrup, turn the heat up and bring to the boil.
4   Once the syrup is bubbling, take the pan off the heat. Mash the fruit up a bit, then cover with a lid and leave to stand until cold.
5   Add the brandy, stir well and pour into a very large sterilised jar with a tight-fitting lid. Label and leave for two to three months.
6   At the end of the waiting time, strain through a sieve lined with a clean cloth or a piece of muslin and decant into small, sterilised bottles. Adjust the consistency by adding a little more brandy to the liqueur.

Coffee Brandy

Coffee brandy is great spooned over ice cream (as is Baileys) and can also be used to add a bit of oomph to rich chocolate or fruit cakes and puddings. Last year I poured it over the Christmas pudding and it was yummy, although the liqueur couldn't be lit in the same way as a neat spirit.

4fl oz (120ml) brandy
2oz (50g) soft brown sugar
1 tablespoon vanilla extract
2 teaspoons instant coffee granules

1 Put the brandy into a measuring jug; add the sugar, vanilla extract and coffee granules, then top up with hot, previously boiled water to the 1 pint (570ml) mark and stir well.
2 Pour into a saucepan and warm very slowly over a low heat for about 20 minutes until all the sugar has dissolved, stirring occasionally.
3 Allow the coffee brandy to cool completely, then pour straight into a sterilised bottle and label. Can be used immediately and stored in a cool dark place indefinitely.

Rhubarb and Raisin Rum

Make this with fresh British rhubarb in season or with tinned rhubarb any time.

4oz (110g) raisins
1 tin of rhubarb in syrup or 1lb (450g) rhubarb
2oz (50g) granulated sugar (or more)
½ bottle dark rum

1. Wash the raisins in warm water and put in a large saucepan with the tinned rhubarb and extra sugar. If you're using fresh, top and tail the rhubarb, remove stringy bits, cut into chunks and use three times the amount of sugar.

2. Bring to the boil over a low heat, stirring occasionally, until all the sugar dissolves. Simmer gently for 15 minutes, then take the pan off the heat and leave to cool for an hour or two.

3. Add the rum, stir well and pour into a very large sterilised jar with a tight-fitting lid. Label and leave for two to three months.

4. After the waiting time, strain through a clean cloth or piece of muslin. The fruit will have absorbed a lot of the liquid, so for best results be patient and leave the liqueur to drip slowly.

5. Decant into small, sterilised bottles and label. Adjust the consistency by adding a little more rum to the liqueur.

Sloe Gin

Sloe gin is an ancient and traditionally very British recipe, which is reason enough to include it here, even if sloes aren't as readily available as the other fruits in this section. In fact, sloes – the small, bitter wild plums from the blackthorn bush – are often to be found growing in between other plants and shrubs in towns and city parks, as well as in the countryside. If you're one of those people who gets an extra kick out of foraging their food for free, keep a lookout and you're bound to find sloes sooner or later, wherever you live.

Ideally, sloes should be gathered after the first frost, otherwise pick in October or early November to give them time to ripen. Gently rub the sloes clean in a dry cloth or paper towels to remove loose dirt, prick with a needle and freeze until ready to use. (Thaw the sloes before making the liqueur.)

Although sloe gin is ready to drink after steeping for a couple of months, if you wait longer – up to a year even – the flavour intensifies and the result is a more mellow liqueur.

1lb (450g) sloes
½lb (225g) granulated sugar
1½ pints (850ml) gin

1   Put the clean sloes in a very large sterilised jar with the sugar
    and gin. Seal the jar with a tight-fitting lid and shake well.
2   Label and leave for two to three months, giving the jar a good
    shake every day.
3   Strain through a sieve lined with a clean cloth or piece of muslin
    and decant into a sterilised bottle.

Plum Whisky

The kernels inside the plum stones taste just like almonds,
so don't leave them out, they add something to the flavour of
the finished liqueur.

Use any plums you like, but you must use cinnamon sticks
rather than the ground spice, which goes into strings in the warm
syrup and settles into sludge at the bottom of the jar.

½lb (225g) plums (plus stones)
1 mug of soft brown sugar
2 cinnamon sticks
½ bottle of whisky

1   Wash the plums, cut into quarters and remove the stones. Break
    open the stones by placing them between two layers of greaseproof
    paper, clingfilm or an old clean tea towel and bashing them with
    a heavy rolling pin. Remove the kernels – don't worry if they're
    broken – and discard the rest of the stone.
2   Put the sugar and 1 mug of cold water in a large saucepan and heat
    very slowly until all the sugar has dissolved, then add the plums,
    kernels and cinnamon sticks to the syrup and bring to the boil.

3   As soon as the syrup is bubbling, take the pan off the heat and leave to cool down for an hour or two.
4   Add the whisky to the cool fruit and syrup and stir well. When completely cold, pour into a very large sterilised jar with a tight-fitting lid, label and leave for two or three months.
5   Strain through a sieved lined with a clean cloth or piece of muslin, and decant into small, sterilised bottles. Adjust the consistency by adding a little more whisky to the liqueur.

Strawberry Vodka

Also try raspberries or a mixture of soft red fruit. Fruit-flavoured vodkas have a beautiful colour and make great cocktail ingredients.

> 4oz (110g) granulated sugar
> ½lb (225g) sweet British strawberries
> ¼ pint (150ml) vodka

1   Put the sugar and 4fl oz (120ml) cold water in a small saucepan over a low heat for about 20 to 30 minutes until all the sugar has dissolved. Don't bring to the boil; the sugar syrup should be warm but not hot.
2   Slightly squash the strawberries in a bowl, pour over the warm syrup, then leave to cool completely.
3   Pour the fruit and syrup into a large sterilised jar, add the vodka and shake gently.
4   Label and leave for two to three months, then strain the liquid through a fine sieve lined with a clean cloth or piece of muslin and decant into small, sterilised bottles. Adjust the consistency by adding a little more vodka to the liqueur.

Cold Spiced Red Wine

There are lots of old recipes around for 'hippocras', a general name for red or white wines mixed with sugar and spices meant to aid the digestion, which is why these drinks were served with multiple courses originally, and still make a nice change from a bottle of supermarket plonk with a big meal today.

When you pour the wine back into the bottle at Step 3, save the dregs at the bottom for adding flavour to sauces, casseroles and soups, such as the Beef Pan Pie (see page 127), Pork in Plum Sauce (see page 99) or even gravy made with instant granules.

> 1 bottle of French red table wine
> 1 cardamom pod
> 2oz (50g) soft brown sugar
> 2 teaspoons ground cinnamon
> 4–6 cloves
> 1 star anise
> pinch of cayenne pepper

1   Pour the bottle of wine into a clear glass jug, or something similar.
2   Bash the cardamom pod to release the seeds, then add the sugar and all the spices to the wine, stirring well for a couple of minutes.
3   Cover the jug with a saucer or piece of clingfilm and leave to stand at room temperature for at least two hours, until the liquid has cleared and you can see the sediment settled at the bottom.
4   Use a slotted spoon to remove the cardamom pod, cloves and star anise from the wine.
5   Carefully pour the wine back into the bottle, apart from the last inch or so of sludge, which keeps for up to three days in the fridge and can be added to any number of sauces (see above). The hippocras is best made freshly and enjoyed the same day.

Toffee Vodka

Do-it-yourself toffee vodka recipes abound, including a students' one that uses toffee-flavoured ice cream syrup, and one where you have to dissolve a lump of toffee in the vodka...

Anyway, toffee vodka is very simple and can be made by absolutely anyone with a couple of basic ingredients. The result is a clear, additive-free, golden brown spirit with no sediment. And better still, there's no waiting involved.

> 1 mug of soft brown sugar
> 1½ pints (850ml) vodka

1   Put the sugar and ½ mug of cold water in a large saucepan and heat *very* slowly for about half an hour until all the sugar has dissolved.
2   Pour the syrup into a large measuring jug and leave to cool completely.
3   Once the syrup is cool, pour vodka into the jug up to the 2 pint (1.25 litre) mark and stir well to blend the syrup and spirit completely.
4   Bottle and drink as soon as you like.

Irish Cream

There's nothing quite like Baileys, but when you don't have the real thing, this homemade Irish cream liqueur won't let you down.

An Irishman recently told me that another Irishman, James Bailey, invented this liqueur for the benefit of women who want to drink alcohol but don't like the taste, so perhaps it's no coincidence that the innocent creamy sweetness belies the fact that it's actually a pretty strong drink.

Real Baileys is made with Irish whisky of course, but I always use the supermarket's cheaper own-brand Scotch for the cheat's version and it works like a charm. Give it a try. It's good. It's really good. Also try the Baileys Cream Pie on page 60.

½ pint (275ml) whisky
1 tin (397g) condensed milk
1 carton (300ml/10fl oz) whipping cream
3 egg whites
2 tablespoons chocolate syrup
2 teaspoons instant coffee dissolved in 1 tablespoon hot water
2 teaspoons vanilla extract

1   Put all the ingredients into a food processor or blender (2 litres plus) and whiz for a minute till smooth.
2   Keep in a bottle with a tight lid for up to two weeks and serve with lots of ice.

cook's tip

- To make a milkshake, mix half a glass of the Irish Cream with half a glass of fresh milk and liquidize with a couple of big scoops of crushed ice. (Serve in your best highball glasses with black bendy straws to make it yummy.)
- Alternatively, garnish with thin edible chocolate 'straws' like Mikado or extra long Matchmakers, or customise with a few drops of peppermint, orange or vanilla extract, according to taste.
- Finish with a light dusting of two parts cocoa powder mixed with one part icing sugar.

Non-alcoholic drinks

Making the simplest, family-friendly drinks is another one of those things I remember from childhood, and because most kids enjoy producing anything they can eat or drink – mine used to love standing on a kitchen chair squeezing oranges on our tiny, low-tech electric juicer – this is something else you can have a go at together.

For an instant and almost homemade drink with absolutely no waiting involved, there's Ice Cream Soda: One scoop of vanilla ice cream in a tall, plastic tumbler, topped up with sparkling soda water and served with a straw and a long spoon. And St Clements: Equal parts of orange juice and bitter lemon, or lemonade and a couple of big splashes of bottled lemon juice. Garnish with orange and apple slices.

Rosehip Syrup

A spoonful of rosehip syrup was regularly given to babies and toddlers as a tonic when I was a child, and it's surely a custom worth reviving, despite the heavy sugar content, because rosehips are packed with vitamin C. Not only that, the syrup is very versatile and can be diluted with water and taken as a drink (approximately 1 part syrup to 5 parts water) or poured over pancakes, ice cream, sponge and milk puddings or cheesecake. It can also be used as a hangover cure (see page 212). Rosehips are soft, ripe and ready for picking in October and November.

½lb (225g) rosehips
2–3 cloves
1 cinnamon stick
4oz (110g) granulated sugar

1. Wash and crush the rosehips and put in a large saucepan with the cloves, cinnamon and 1 pint (570ml) water. Bring to the boil and simmer for 15 to 20 minutes.
2. Strain through a sieve, then return the liquid to the pan with the sugar and heat slowly until the sugar has dissolved. Bring to the boil again and simmer gently for another 10 minutes.
3. Allow the syrup to cool completely, then pour into small, sterilised bottles. Keeps in the fridge for at least one week or for many months if un-opened.

Lemon Barley Water

4oz (110g) pearl barley
2–3 lemons
2oz (50g) sugar

1. Put the pearl barley in a sieve and rinse through with cold water. Put in a small saucepan, just cover with fresh cold water, bring to the boil and simmer for 5 minutes.
2. Strain the barley and rinse through with cold water a second time.
3. Put the barley in a large heatproof jug (2½ pints/1.5 litres) and add the finely grated rind of all the lemons.
4. Pour on 2 pints (1.25 litres) boiling water, then add the sugar to the jug, stirring occasionally while it dissolves. Cover with a cloth and leave to cool.
5. When the liquid is cold, add the juice of the lemons, strain into clean containers and store in the fridge. Dilute the lemon barley water with still or fizzy water as and when it's served.

Old-fashioned Apple Juice

This recipe makes about 6 litres from one bag of apples. You can't drink it for a couple of weeks, but the method is so satisfyingly simple and the ingredients so cheap, I think it's worth the wait. It's also a good one for kids to try on their own during long holidays or whenever they're bored and complaining that you never let them do anything interesting blah blah blah.

By the end of the first week, you'll be able to detect a lovely cidery scent whenever you stir the apples, leaving you with the impression that you're doing something rather more spectacular than mixing fruit and tap water together in a bucket. Reduce the amount of sugar by about a quarter if you prefer your juice a lot less sweet, and halve the amount of sugar if you want it tart and a little bit tangy.

> 4½lb (2kg) Bramley cooking apples (approx)
> 2lb (900g) granulated or soft brown sugar
> zest and juice of 3 lemons

1   Remove the stalks and wipe the apples to get rid of any loose dirt, then cut the fruit into big chunks, skin, core, pips and all.
2   Crush everything up with a potato masher or take the easy route and whiz the fruit in the food processor in small batches for a few seconds at a time to make a very rough purée.
3   In a 10-litre bucket with a tight-fitting lid, put the mashed up fruit with 10 pints (5.75 litres) fresh cold water, stir well, then close the lid and leave to stand for 10 days, stirring well every morning and evening.
4   Line a second 10-litre bucket with an old clean cotton pillowcase – or a proper jelly bag if you have one – and strain the apple mixture through the cloth into the new bucket. Squeeze gently to get the liquid out more quickly.
5   Add the sugar and the finely grated zest and juice from the lemons to the cider, stir well, cover with the lid again and leave to stand for 24 hours.

6 Strain the cider once more, then use a jug or a funnel to pour it into three 3½-pint (2-litre) screw-top bottles. Label the bottles and leave for one week before drinking. The flavour improves the longer you leave it and the juice can be kept unrefrigerated for quite a few months.

Elderflower Cordial

This recipe was given to me by Sam Finlay, who makes her elderflower cordial from the Traditional Elderflower Cordial recipe on Fiona Nevile's wonderful Cottage Smallholder website. You can find elderflowers growing in the hedgerows every spring and very early summer if you live in or near the countryside, so whenever you make this cordial, make masses and share some of it with your less privileged city friends. It's very versatile and they'll love you for it. (Citric acid can be bought from the chemist.)

> 2lb (900g) granulated sugar
> 4 lemons
> 20 large elderflower heads (that's the *whole* heads,
>   not the individual flowers)
> 2oz (50g) citric acid

1 Pour 2 pints (1.25 litres) boiling water over the sugar; stir well and leave to cool, stirring occasionally to dissolve the sugar. Meanwhile, zest the lemons into a small bowl, then cut them in half, squeeze the juice into the bowl, pips and all, and throw the skins in too.

2 Once the water is cool, add the elderflowers, citric acid and all the lemon. Cover and leave for 48 hours.

3 Strain the liquid *twice* through a sieve lined with a clean piece of muslin and pour into sterilised bottles.

4 Dilute the cordial, approximately 5 to 6 parts water to 1 part cordial, as you would with any other concentrated syrup.

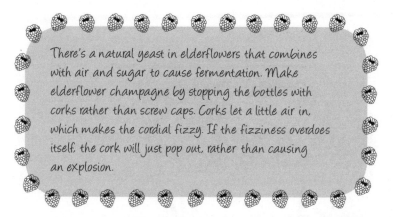

There's a natural yeast in elderflowers that combines with air and sugar to cause fermentation. Make elderflower champagne by stopping the bottles with corks rather than screw caps. Corks let a little air in, which makes the cordial fizzy. If the fizziness overdoes itself, the cork will just pop out, rather than causing an explosion.

Preserves

There are dozens of old recipes around for chutneys, jams,
butters and bottled fruits. These four are the simplest, and
I know they work, so they're the perfect starting point if you've
never preserved anything before, but want to give it a go.

Simple Strawberry Jam

I'm not a great one for recipes that make you wait (liqueurs and rum pots excepted) and this one takes almost three days. But because it's so simple and there's something reassuringly slummy about leaving a big bowl of sweet-smelling strawberries and sugar sitting around in the kitchen for a couple of days, the whole process is actually quite pleasurable.

The only slightly tricky part is knowing when the jam has reached setting point, and even this isn't difficult if you know what you're looking for. Once the syrup is noticeably thicker, the fruit has broken down and the jam is a slightly darker red, test it by taking the pan off the heat and transferring a teaspoonful of jam onto a cold plate. Push the jam with the back of the spoon and if it gels and bunches up in a couple of seconds, it's ready. Don't expect the jam to look 'finished' in the pan, you really need to see it on the plate to be able to tell, and if you leave it boiling for too long it turns brown and sticky in a matter of minutes, by which time it will be too late. Have the courage of your convictions and trust this simple little recipe to work.

Makes about 2 jam jars
2lb (900g) strawberries
2lb (900g) jam sugar

1   Hull the strawberries (cut very large ones in half but leave the rest whole) and layer the fruit in a big china or Pyrex bowl with all the sugar. Cover with a plate or a piece of clingfilm and leave overnight.
2   Empty the entire contents of the bowl into a very large pan (don't bother rinsing the bowl), bring to the boil and boil steadily for 5 minutes. Tip everything back into the bowl and once the fruit has cooled, cover the bowl again and leave overnight a second time.
3   Empty the bowl into the pan, as before, bring to the boil and boil steadily for about 30 to 40 minutes until the jam reaches setting point (see above), stirring occasionally.

4   Leave the jam in the pan for about 15 minutes, then carefully spoon it into clean, warm jars to cool down. When cold, put a circle of greaseproof paper or waxed paper on top of the jam, then screw the lid on the jar and label.

Blackberry Chutney

This is good with any hot roasted meat, especially duck and pork, or in sandwiches with cold chicken or ham.

This quantity will fill approximately 2 jam jars
2lb (900g) blackberries
1lb (450g) apples
1lb (450g) onions
½ pint (275ml) malt vinegar
1 teaspoon salt
1 teaspoon ground ginger
1 teaspoon mustard powder
½ teaspoon nutmeg
¼ teaspoon cayenne pepper
5oz (150g) soft brown sugar

1   Put the washed blackberries in a large pan with the peeled and chopped apples and onions.
2   Put the rest of the ingredients *except for the sugar* in the pan, bring to the boil and simmer gently for an hour.
3   Strain through a large sieve over a bowl, leaving the liquid to drip through the sieve for about an hour, gently pressing the pulp in the sieve from time to time to help it along.
4   Put the pulp back into the pan with all the sugar and bring to the boil again before simmering gently for another half an hour or so, until the chutney is thick and looks right to you.
5   Take the pan off the heat and allow to cool for a while before spooning the chutney into clean, warm jars.

Spicy Apple Butter

This is a more elaborate apple sauce of the kind you'd normally eat with roast pork or another strong-flavoured meat, like duck or venison. I often mix apple sauce – or tinned apples when I'm cheating – in with the meat for sausage rolls. You can also mix this apple butter with mincemeat, peaches or apricots in pies and crumbles, or even serve it hot over ice cream. Mix different types of apples, including windfalls and crab apples.

Makes approximately two jam jars
4lb (1.75kg) apples
1 pint cider
½ teaspoon ground cloves
½ teaspoon ground cinnamon
½ teaspoon nutmeg
granulated or soft brown sugar

1   Clean the apples and cut into large pieces, but do not peel or core them.
2   In a very large saucepan or preserving pan, simmer the apples in 1 pint (570ml) water and the cider for about 20 minutes until soft (put the fruit in the cold liquid and bring to the boil first), then strain off excess liquid.
3   Push the apples through a sieve so only the skins and pips are left behind, then weigh the apple pulp and mix the fruit with approximately 10oz (275g) sugar for every 1lb (450g) fruit.
4   Put the fruit back in the pan with the spices and cook gently, stirring frequently, until thick.
5   Pour the apple butter into warm sterilised jars while the fruit is still warm, and cover with a circle of waxed paper or very lightly greased baking parchment. Put the lids on tightly once the fruit is cold. Label and eat within three months.

Rum Pot

A rum pot, or *rumtopf*, is a German dessert, traditionally eaten at Christmas. Ideally, the fruit needs to soak for about three months, but if you get your rum pot started in early summer, there's no reason why you can't use some of the fruit and replace it throughout the season, making sure the pot's full again at the beginning of autumn so the fruit can mature properly in time for winter.

Unless you already have the real thing, any earthenware container or a very large glass jar with a heavy lid is good for making a rum pot. Experiment with different kinds of berries and soft fruits. Strawberries, raspberries, redcurrants, plums, cherries, blueberries, apricots, peaches and nectarines are all good for rum pots. Citrus fruits, apples, pears and bananas don't work. Eat the fruit with ice cream and yoghurt or mix with the same quantity of fresh (or tinned) fruit in pies and crumbles.

> 4lb (1.75kg) fruit (approx)
> 4lb (1.75kg) granulated sugar
> 1 bottle of rum, light or dark

1 Use only whole, ripe fruit without bruises. Hull the strawberries, but no need to remove cherry or plum stones, unless you want to. Leave berries whole and cut larger fruit into slices or chunks. Don't immerse the fruit in water; clean it by wiping with a very clean, damp cloth.

2 Layer the fruit in the clean, dry crock with the same weight of sugar and pour on the rum. Don't stir. Cover with waxed paper or very lightly oiled baking parchment, put the lid on and store in a cool, dark place.

3 Wait two or three weeks before taking fruit from the jar and keep adding fruit in season to the rum pot to replace what you use.

cook's tip

You can buy waxed paper from some kitchen shops, but a double layer of greaseproof or baking parchment wiped over with a little sunflower oil will do.

Acknowledgements

A very big thank you to Jon and Claire Hack, Barbara Holcombe, Debbie Finlay, Sam Finlay, Patricia Stockham, Fiona Nevile, Maddie Richardson, Caroline Green and Rose Prince for giving me recipe ideas, tips, advice and inspiration; also to my teenage volunteers: Annabelle and Rachel Todd, Amy Tyler, Jess Sinyor, Matt Weatherley and Oliver, Billy and Eleanor Holcombe, who cooked some of the recipes in order to prove they really are as easy as all that. I'm especially grateful to Eleanor for organising the index, to Zelda Turner who commissioned the book in the first place and Kay Halsey for the brilliant edit; also Sarah Hammond, Nicky Ross and everyone else at Hodder & Stoughton. And not forgetting my very good friend Carole Moore, who's always ready to taste and try out recipes, and generally talk about food for hours at a time. If she ever gets fed up with it, she's much too nice to let me know.

Index

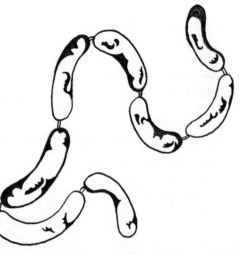